PEOPLE

*Tapping the Spirit of
Quality Performance and
Service in Your Organization*

POWER

Thomas J.
Stevenin, Ph.D.

PEOPLE

Tapping the Spirit of Quality Performance and Service in Your Organization

POWER

Thomas J. Stevenin, Ph.D.

ISBN: 1-881273-55-5

1 3 5 7 9 10 8 6 4 2

Printed in the United States of America

To Nettie

ACKNOWLEDGMENTS

This book is based on thirty years of experience in organizational life. In that time I've worked for and with some of the finest managers and employees in America. Their willingness to share themselves with me and to help me grow has contributed immeasurably to my thinking and development. The consulting business has been a magic carpet that has taken me to Japan, Russia, Lithuania, Canada, and Costa Rica. I've been enriched by managers and workers in these countries.

I've also been blessed by wonderful colleagues in the consulting profession. John Schuster, Jack Knuth, Patricia Kane, Norma Boyer, Trudy Short, Dennis Landis, Patrick Handley, and a host of others have helped me grow personally and professionally. There's nothing greater than to spend your life advancing causes you believe in with colleagues you respect and admire.

Thanks especially to my Executive Assistant and Manager of Consulting Services, Trish Ayers, for her preparation of the manuscript. Thanks also to my colleagues Doug Hundley, Melissa and Michael Ashcraft, and Norma Boyer, who contributed ideas to the text and assisted with the editing. Thanks, as well, to Anne Scherich, of Moody Press, for her final editing of this project.

Finally, thanks to my beloved wife of twenty-eight years, Barbara, who is a great encourager and positive reinforcer. I must also mention our adopted three-year-old, Ian. When I come home from a long trip, sometimes tired and discouraged, he runs full tilt down the walk, leaps into my arms, and says, "I love you, Papa." That's my reminder of the importance of affirmation and the nourishment of the inner spirit.

TABLE OF CONTENTS

INTRODUCTION

I've spent much of my life studying how to work with people. I've noticed that not everyone knows how.

Although most of the examples I use in this book come from business, the principles discussed have no bounds. Wherever you find yourself working with other people—a business, a nonprofit group, a government agency, a church or temple, wherever—this book will help you improve the way people work together in your organization.

Early on, when I was a sales representative, I came under the tutelage of Walter. Walter taught me everything he knew about selling and also how to work with the likes of me. At the time, I didn't really want to be in sales, and I lacked many of the skills needed to be successful. One day, Walter accompanied me on my calls. He observed me as I called on about a dozen customers. At the end of the day, we went to a quiet place and talked.

Walter praised me extravagantly. "Tom," he said, "that was great today. You have wonderful rapport with people. You are great at getting people into conversations." I was gratified to hear this, since I had been up all night preparing for these calls and thought I might lose my job if Walter was not sold on me. "Now there's just one thing," Walter said. "I kept hoping all day that you could work in a reference to the products we sell."

Walter took out a pen, grabbed a napkin, and outlined how to open a sale. Then he taught me something more important. He took out his pocket calendar, wrote a note to himself in the calendar, and showed the note to me. "Make calls with Tom," the note read. "Notice how he has improved in his ability to open a sale."

Walter comes to mind because many people in the United States do not know how to notice improvement. They want improvement. They want people with whom they work to improve. They may even be participating in a quality program that promises improvement. Still, not all quality programs have brought about fundamental change. In fact, recent reports estimate that about 60 percent of quality programs have not taken hold or have resulted in only temporary improvement.

I have seen quality programs at work in many organizations and have helped implement more than one hundred successful quality programs. I believe these programs are vital to our nation's well-being and to the well-being of those people who are participating in them, willingly or unwillingly. They can fundamentally change the way people work with one another. I believe that quality programs do work—but that something essential is missing in many of them.

What's missing is an understanding of the source of quality. The source about which I write in this book is not a program in itself. It cannot be installed or instilled. But it can be tapped. It is a kind of spirit, intangible but real.

Years ago, I knew a woman who knew how to tap the inner spirit. Her name was Nettie. She taught fourth grade at a small, neighborhood school. She wore a black skirt and white blouse and combed her hair once a day if she thought about it. What she thought about most were her students. She loved teaching, and she loved her students.

One of her more challenging students was a boy who had not yet learned to write his name correctly. In those days, he was called Tommy. When the boy was asked to write his name, he would get the letters turned around and would always leave out one *M*. He came to be known as "YMOT." Many people thought "YMOT" was his real name. Today, we call his condition "dyslexia." In those days, it was called "dumb." He also had a short attention span and was hyperactive. After the third grade, the school sent a note home to the boy's parents: "Please don't send YMOT back to this school again. He will never finish a normal elementary school program. He is severely retarded."

The boy's parents did send him back, nevertheless, and he was face-to-face with Nettie. During the second week of classes, Nettie asked the boy to stay in during recess. The other boys and girls in the class went outside as Nettie sat down at a little desk beside the boy. "I asked you to stay in because I have something important to tell you," she said. "You have a wonderful mind."

The astonished boy looked at his teacher. "Have you seen my record?" he asked.

"No, I never look at a student's record before he comes to me," she said. "Besides, it doesn't mean a thing. After all, he hasn't had me yet!"

Nettie told the boy that she believed he could write his name correctly and that she would work with him every day during recess, at noon, and after school. "If you write your name correctly six times out of ten at the end of the semester, I'll give you an A in all subjects," she said. She gave him incredible amounts of praise and encouragement.

The boy tried. But despite his best efforts, he couldn't write his name correctly six times out of ten at the end of the semester.

"Don't be discouraged," Nettie told the boy. "You have a wonderful mind. I notice you don't live far away from me. Come over on Saturdays, and we'll take an extra hour. We'll have the same goal next semester."

And so, week after week for yet another semester, the boy worked at spelling his name correctly. Sometimes it went well. Sometimes it went badly. The boy remembers one Saturday in Nettie's kitchen when he was so frustrated that he pounded his head on Nettie's Formica® table and stained it with blood. At the end of that semester, though, the boy could spell his name correctly, not six times out of ten, but ten times out of ten: "TOMMY." He got an A in every subject.

The next year, Tommy returned to the same school. When he walked into the fifth-grade class, he thought he had made another mistake, for standing at the front of the class was Nettie. It was the only time in forty years that she ever taught fifth grade. The boy was, again, one of her students. He never knew why. In later life, he came to wonder if perhaps God had worked it out just for him.

I was that boy. Everything I've ever done, I owe to my fourth and fifth grade teacher, Nettie Weidenmann. She tapped something in me that changed the way I thought about myself. She opened the door to a quality life and quality work. She tapped the source, the inner spirit.

You can, too.

1

THE CUSTOMER

◣

Serving the Inner Spirit

When was the last time someone behaved as though he couldn't do without you? When was the last time a company acted as though it couldn't do without your business? Why is the quality movement in serious trouble in America? Because the movement consistently tends to forget human beings—two human beings in particular—the customer and the employee.

Let's talk first about the customer.

Chances are, you work for an organization that already has some sort of quality program. Three-fourths of organizations in the United States do. But the flaw in most of these quality programs is that the organization defines its own quality. It doesn't define quality by the one person who really knows if it is present: the customer.

Some time ago I went into a convenience store to buy six big apples. I fumbled with the apples as I walked to the front of the store to pay for them. At the cash register was a woman whose makeup made her look as if she was spoiling. Her customer skills certainly were. She was talking on the phone and seemed annoyed that I had interrupted her conversation.

"You want a sack for those?" she asked me, with some disdain.

"No," I said, "Just give me a stick, and I'll roll them out the door." How would anyone carry six apples without a sack?

Contrast that woman's behavior with the behavior of the registrar of a small hotel on the southern coast of Japan where I once stayed. He was checking me in when I realized that I had left my briefcase at the hotel I had stayed in the night before, which was in a city several hours away. I needed the materials in the briefcase for a presentation I was to make the next day.

"What was the name of the hotel?" the registrar asked. I told him.

"Do you remember your room number?" he asked. I did, and I gave it to him.

"Please don't worry, Dr. Stevenin," he said. "We will take care of this."

Within a few minutes, an employee rushed out of the hotel to get my briefcase. The registrar had called the hotel where I had left it and made arrangements for its delivery. Within a few hours, it was in my room. And the hotel employee wouldn't accept a tip.

The registrar behaved as though his hotel could not do without me. He understood that his job was to focus on me. His interaction with me was a *relationship*, not a simple transaction.

The best quality products in the world are made in the United States. Where America lags behind is in customer service, the communication and follow-up that accompanies the product or service.

CUSTOMER SERVICE MEANS SERVING

Not long ago I worked with a church that was trying to increase its outreach and touch more lives. They decided to spend more than forty thousand dollars remodeling the nursery. They also hired a professional child care staff. A waste of money? Absolutely not. They found that many young couples start searching for faith after they have children. When they visit a church, they don't know much about creeds but they do know a lot about children. They want to know their children are secure while they attend adult classes or worship.

This same church has the ten best parking spots "Reserved for Visitors." Their theme is "We want to be your friend." Everything about the place says, "We care about you. We want to help you. You are special to us!"

QUALITY AND PROFITS

If you are running a business, you have an added incentive to operate this way. The Strategic Planning Institute in Cambridge, Massachusetts, in cooperation with the Harvard Business School, conducted a study, *Profit Impact of Marketing Strategy*, of over 3,000 strategic business units in 450 firms over an eighteen-year time frame. They found that when the customer's perception of a business's quality ranked in the top fifth of those in its industry, the company achieved pre-tax returns on investment, on average, of about 32 percent a year. When quality was perceived as in the bottom 40 percent, return on investment averaged 14 percent less. The conclusion of the Harvard study: "High profits correlate better with customer-perceived quality than with any other variable."[1]

The Commerce Department's National Institute of Standards and Technology (NIST) "invested" a hypothetical $1,000 in each of the five publicly traded, whole company winners of the Malcolm Baldrige National Quality Award and the parent companies of seven subsidiary winners. The success of the investment was tracked from the first business day in April of the year the company won the award (or the date it went public) to October 3, 1994. Adjustments were made for stock splits and/or stock dividends. Another hypothetical $1,000 was invested in the Standard & Poor's 500 at the same time.

NIST found that the five whole company winners—Eastman Chemical Company, Federal Express, Motorola, Solectron, and Zytec Corporation—outperformed the S&P 500 by 6.5 to 1, a 188 percent return on investment compared to a 28 percent return for the S&P 500.

The results were similar for the seven publicly traded parent companies—Westinghouse Electric, Xerox, General Motors, IBM, AT&T, and Texas Instruments. They showed a 92 percent return on investment, compared to a 33 percent return for the S&P 500—better by almost 3 to 1. Other independent studies have shown similar results.

Although quality management cannot guarantee success, Malcolm Baldrige award winners report many improvements as a result of investing in quality management:

- Ko Nishimura, president and chief executive officer of Solectron Corporation, reports that the company continues to use the Malcolm Baldrige National Quality Award criteria even after winning the award in 1991. These criteria have helped to build a quality company and return substantial value to their shareholders. In the last five years, sales have increased from $130 million to $1.457 billion, net profit has increased from $4 million to $56 million, and the stock price has had an average growth of 82 percent per year.

- Another winner, Marlow Industries, reports that through the Baldrige criteria it has developed a wide variety of quality tools and put into place a quality system that has resulted in successful penetration of new markets and a sales increase of 34 percent in one year.

- Quality management at the Ritz-Carlton Hotels has helped the company eliminate $75 million in waste through project improvements.

- Ames Rubber Corporation reports that sharing quality management techniques with its suppliers has helped it to achieve a 99.9 percent quality and on-time delivery status.

- Cumulative manufacturing cost savings at Motorola, a 1988 winner, for 1987 through the second quarter of 1994 were more than $5.5 billion.[2]

POOR QUALITY IS COSTLY

Conversely, nothing is more costly than a lack of quality. A recent survey of the customers of fourteen major companies showed that only 15 percent of the customers switched their business to a competitor because they found a better product, and only 15 percent switched because they found a cheaper product. Twenty percent switched because they had experienced too little contact and individual attention. The largest number—

45 percent—said they switched because the attention they did receive was of poor quality.[3]

It costs five times as much to replace a typical customer as it does to take actions that would keep the customer in the first place. Companies that do not recognize the needs of their customers spend millions on sales and marketing just to replace the customers they're losing.

Recently a bank customer in a major city withdrew $8 million in cash, securities, and investments. He had a large family trust account, a good-sized commercial account, and a small personal checking account, which he and his spouse occasionally overdrew. Three times he called the bank and said: "If you send me one more Insufficient Funds Notice and fine me twenty-five dollars when in fact I have over eight million dollars in your bank, I'm going to come and get it!" Now you know what happened.

The following week I visited the president of the bank, who had decided this would be an excellent time to begin a quality program. The most interesting thing he said was this: "Our people didn't think it was a serious problem because we were treating him just like any other customer." I pointed out that that was precisely the problem. He wasn't like any other customer. In fact, no customer is.

PROCESSING VERSUS PLEASING

The bank reflects a common problem in organizations today. It had set up an automated system to handle customers but couldn't figure out how to intervene in its own system. The problem with most large-scale customer service systems today is that they are set up to *process* people, not to *please* them. There's an enormous difference!

We actually train people to process customers, not please them. This is in contrast to many companies abroad. Richard Whitely, in *The Customer-Driven Company*, relates this incident from his travels.

Recently I arrived at the front desk of a prestigious Chicago hotel to check in. While the clerk looked for my reservation, I noticed hotel staff members setting up microphones and speakers nearby. They appeared to be getting ready for some kind of musical performance. A frustrating dialogue ensued.

"What's going on over there?" I asked the clerk. Hoping for a respite from an exhausting business trip, I wanted to know when the concert would begin.

"I don't know," he said as he went about his business.

"Who would know?" I pressed.

"I don't know," came the reply. "Maybe the assistant manager." The clerk continued methodically punching keys on his computer terminal. He showed no interest in finding the assistant manager or anyone else knowledgeable about the day's schedule of events. I was giving up on the concert, but it seemed bizarre for the hotel to plan a special event and then neglect to inform the staff about it.

After completing the perfunctory check-in, the clerk turned away from the computer, handed me my key, looked me square in the eye, and said in a sincere voice: "Thank you very much, Mr. Whitely. My name is John. If there's anything I can do to help you, please let me know."

Incredulous, I looked at him and said as politely as I could: "John, I just asked you for your help. I'd like to know what they're setting up for over there."

Then, and only then, did the light go on for John. I was right— it was a concert organized explicitly for the enjoyment of the hotel's customers.

Whitely concludes by making this point:

John had obviously received training. Otherwise, how would he know he was supposed to say, "If there's anything I can do to help you, please let me know"? But the training taught John to process customers, not to please them. John processed me flawlessly by some standards [but] John's manager hadn't helped him understand the distinction between his job of following a script and his job of creating a happy customer. As a result, although the check-in procedure was technically perfect, the customer was not well served.[4]

THE INTERNAL CUSTOMER

Most organizations are designed for the needs of the organization, not for the needs of the persons being served by the organization. Even most companies' measures of quality tend to be company-defined, not customer-defined. Yet the customer defines quality in his or her terms—not management's terms. No organization can measure itself accurately if it does not take that into account.

That is why the popular "Internal Customer" concept is flawed. It says that everyone in an organization should serve either the external customer or someone inside the company who in turn serves the customer. But if you have someone who serves someone who serves someone who serves the customer, you've got too many layers. You've created a bureaucracy and have removed yourself from the only real customer—the external customer, the end user.

QUALITY IS A PASSION

Total quality can't be just a program or even a process. It must be a passion. Westinghouse chairman John C. Marous describes this passion: "Total quality is everything, it's everybody. And it is almost like a religion. To have total quality you're going to have to change your culture. You can't change your culture without an emotional experience."

Total quality organizations have an incredibly high goal—to do the right thing for 100 percent of the customers 100 percent of the time. Does that seem unrealistic? Isn't 99 percent good enough? Just think what you'd get if 99 percent were good enough in certain areas.

- No electric service for fifteen minutes each day
- 1.7 million pieces of first-class mail lost each day
- 35,000 newborn babies dropped by doctors or nurses each year
- 200,000 people getting the wrong drug prescriptions each year
- Three misspelled words on the average page of type
- 2 million people dying from food poisoning each year

The truth is that we often demand 100 percent of ourselves. We don't get lost driving home and end up at the wrong house 8 percent of the time. We don't think it's OK to miss 98 percent of the other cars on the road and hit only 2 percent. We want 100 percent in those areas. That's the difference between being good and being great, between all right and excellent, between a processed customer and a pleased customer. Our goal should be nothing less than doing the right thing for the people we serve 100 percent of the time!

QUALITY COMPANIES

In the last few years, a handful of companies have begun vital transformations into a new, rare breed of organization. They provide high quality, not according to definitions they've developed on their own, but *as the customer defines it.* And they achieve that quality in two dimensions—the quality of the product or service itself and the quality of customer communications and follow-up.

Quality is a religion at Federal Express. The company inspires its employees to go to extraordinary lengths to serve the customer. One example: When communications equipment in Boston failed during the Labor Day holiday in 1986, the company's trace department in Memphis couldn't confirm the location of a package of blood for Children's Hospital in Boston. The rare blood was needed for a life-saving operation the next morning.

An hourly wage employee was called at home. He made a special trip to the building where Federal Express stored material to be delivered but found the lock on the fence had been changed; his key didn't work. He scaled the barbed-wire fence, explained the problem to the security guard, found the package, chartered a private flight, and delivered it. He was named Employee of the Year.

No wonder that in 1990, Federal Express became the first major service company to win the Malcolm Baldrige National Quality Award.

Here's the sad part—in many companies today, that same kind of initiative and decision making by a rank-and-file employee would get him or her fired.

Ritz-Carlton Hotels, another Baldrige winner, has this statement of core values: "If you receive a customer complaint you own that complaint. You are empowered to do whatever is necessary to resolve the complaint to the satisfaction of the customer."

This policy encourages responsibility and ownership of customer satisfaction. It also provides essential feedback for the company.

A study for Travelers Insurance showed that persuading people to complain could be the best business move a company could make. Only 9 percent of the noncomplainers with a gripe involving one hundred dollars or more would buy from the company again. On the other hand, when people did complain and their problems were resolved quickly, an impressive 82 percent would buy again.[5]

Companies that are not customer-focused will lose valuable business, even if their customers do not actually complain. Thousands of customers are insulted, offended, and wronged every day and say nothing. But they do have a secret weapon for getting even—they just take their business elsewhere.[6]

The General Electric owner's manual that comes with any GE appliance lists an 800-number to call for help with any kind of problem. At first, GE worried that it couldn't handle all the calls and thought they would cost too much. But GE is actually saving money and also increasing sales.

How? First, the 800-number gives GE a way of tracking how people use its products and how those products might be improved. And it gives the company a chance to manage complaints. At GE's answer center in Louisville, Kentucky, the specialist who picks up the phone has a personal computer linked to a database with answers to more than 750,000 questions. Let's say you call with a question about a refrigerator. No being put on hold while staff at the center hunt up a refrigerator guru. Instead, the person handling your call brings up facts about your specific model of refrigerator on the PC screen and begins to troubleshoot.

GE has created good will and often avoids a service call and much inconvenience and cost. Listening to the customer is the cheapest and most profitable way to do business. The company estimates that GE spends between $2.50 and $4.50 on a typical call and that the benefits in warranty savings and additional sales are two to three times that.

PUT YOURSELF IN THEIR SHOES

Go to extremes, if you have to, to become customer-focused. As part of their training in professional customer relations, some employees of Meridian BanCorp, in Reading, Pennsylvania, had to fill out deposit slips with Vaseline smeared on their glasses, or count money with three fingers on each hand taped together. The bank wanted to give the employees a better understanding of what older customers with glaucoma or arthritis might be experiencing at the bank.

Chip R. Bell, a senior partner with Performance Research Associates and the author of *Customers as Partners*, said in a recent interview: "Too few recognize that managing object-making (product), with its focus on uniformity and with the customer not a part of the creation process, is very different from managing memory-making (service), with its focus on uniqueness and with the customer partnering in the creation process."[7]

You cannot relate to people in masses. Once you start thinking of people as a "market segment" or a "customer base," you have already lost the essence of quality. The investment firm that affirms its intention to measure success one client at a time has the right vision.

In *Words to Love By*, Mother Teresa writes:

I never look at the masses as my responsibility.

I look at the individual.

I can love only one person at a time.

I can feed only one person at a time.

Just one, one, one.

You get closer to Christ by coming closer to each other.

As Jesus said, "whatever you do to the least of my brethren, you do to me."

So I begin . . . I begin.

I picked up one person,

—maybe if I didn't pick up that one person

I wouldn't have picked up the next 42,000.

The whole work is only a drop in the ocean.

But if I didn't put the drop in, the ocean would be one drop less.
Same thing for you.
Same thing in your family
Same thing in the church where you go,
Just begin . . . one, one, one.[8]

One corporate employee benefits department has this vision statement:

> Benefits are about people. It's not whether you have the forms filled in or whether the checks are written. It's whether individual people are cared for when they're sick, helped when they're in trouble.

That's quality! That's an organization worth giving your professional life to. That's a place where you could go to work in the morning and bring your inner spirit with you.

Who is the key to this kind of excellence in customer-oriented quality? The employees serving them. That leads us to the second overlooked person in the quality equation—our own associates, our employee team. How employees treat customers, serve members, and resolve problems will be a reflection of the treatment they receive. Your first customer is your own employee.

This means much more than reengineering, training, or Total Quality Management programs. If that's all you have going for you, you're not a player. Something must happen to the inner spirit of your employees. They have to bring their spirits to work, must have an inner commitment to excellence. The good news is that they can and they will.

REFERENCES

ADDITIONAL READING

1. Robert D. Buzzell and Bradley T. Gale, *The PIMS Principles: Linking Strategy to Performance* (New York: Free, 1987), 107ff.
2. Ibid.
3. Forum Corporation, *Customer Focus Research Study* (1988), 19.

4. Richard C. Whiteley, *The Customer-Driven Company: Moving From Talk to Action* (Reading, Mass.: Addison Wesley, 1991), 87.

5. *Travelers Tribune Newsletter* (February 1989).

6. White House Office of Consumer Affairs, *Consumer Complaint Handling in America*, 1980.

7. Scott Madison Paton, "New Gurus: The Next Leaders of the Quality Revolution," *Quality Digest* (March 1995), 37.

8. Mother Teresa, *Words to Love By* (Notre Dame, Ind.: Ave Maria, 1983).

2

THE EMPLOYEE

◪

Tapping the Inner Spirit

What most managers don't know about quality programs is that a quality attitude doesn't just happen. A person doesn't get up one morning and say to himself, "OK, today I'm going to do quality work." A quality attitude is the result of behaviors that are encouraged in a way that is meaningful to the employee.

Let's say you are an employee in a business that has a quality program. You have seen some improvement in the business since the program began. Perhaps one of your suggestions contributed to that improvement. Did anyone notice? Did anyone comment on your contribution? Did anyone do anything to make you want to contribute again?

When I began working in the quality field more than thirty years ago, I assumed that if you showed business people how something could be done better, faster, easier, and with fewer errors, they would automatically want to do it that way. I was wrong.

I learned that quality programs can be threatening. Even the idea of improvement can be threatening. Some people think a suggestion for improvement is an implied criticism of the way they are doing their job. Others are uncomfortable with the uncertainty that quality programs create—and quality is by definition not static. It demands that we change to meet our customers' ever-changing needs—sometimes daily.

Quality also demands a radical culture change. I'll never forget standing in an automobile plant a few years ago watching management put up a set of statistical process-control charts. A few minutes later I was astonished to see some angry employees take them down, tear them up, and throw them into the trash. You can't plug a positive program into a negative culture. If the spirit isn't right, nothing else will be right.

TRUST

Recently, the Covey Leadership Center set out to discover the forces that restrained quality and continuous improvement in organizations. Staff from the center interviewed 3,500 individuals in corporations, health care, nonprofit organizations, and government. This was the conclusion of the study:

> The number one identified problem was distrust in senior management. In further analysis, not only did we find that employees distrust senior management, but senior management also distrusts employees. We likewise found that in many organizations, senior management distrusts other senior management!
>
> From our own in-depth leadership development work with senior officers, middle managers and employees in hundreds of different organizations, the single most recurring source of pain people feel within organizations is typically described as, "We don't have a lot of trust around here."[1]

Nevertheless, most of the organizations we work for have not spent much time thinking about how to create a positive culture to motivate employees. Managers have little understanding of how to reward behavior that shows an ongoing commitment to quality, and they have forgotten to focus on the needs of the people who focus on the customer's needs.

Much of this results from myths that have dominated our understanding of human motivation.

Myth: As an executive, I have the power to change other people's attitudes and behaviors.

The truth is that motivation is a door locked from the inside.

Human beings are in charge of their own behavior, and each person's behavior is determined by a unique set of feelings and values.

The only person whose behavior you have complete authority to change is you. But when you make a sincere effort to change your behavior, others will make dramatic changes in their behavior. If you are installing an incentive program, require all key leaders to keep a journal of their behaviors. Ask them to list the number of times per day or week they make positive, reinforcing comments to staff concerning significant improvements in their performance. Make sure you keep a journal of your own as well.

The focus in all motivational systems must be on improvement, not perfection. Performance doesn't get perfect. It gets better. And helping people perform better is what management is all about. If you are helping people improve in the key behaviors that produce results, you are an excellent leader.

Excellent leaders don't run around offering vague, general comments, such as "Keep up the good work." Too many of us do that now. Instead, they tie all praise to specific improvements in performance. They focus on performance, not simply on personality or political skills.

Myth: People are a mystery. You can't figure out what motivates them.

All people are the same in their response to rewards. They differ greatly, however, in what they find rewarding. Some employees love to be praised in public. They thrive on recognition before a group. Shy people, on the other hand, may be embarrassed by public praise. As a leader, you need to know which is which.

People are always telling us what motivates them. The trouble is, we're not listening. Sports buffs are likely to work hard for free tickets to a major sports event. Money-motivated people have high living standards and want cash. They'll burn the midnight oil for a bonus or commission. People who constantly talk about their families will probably enjoy a company-sponsored family event (such as a free weekend in a hotel).

Be creative and try something different. A large midwestern credit union recently wanted to increase members' use of share drafts. An executive placed vases on the desks of seven employees who had a high degree of contact with credit union members. Each time a share draft account was opened, he placed a silk flower in the successful salesperson's vase. Six of the seven employees' performance improved. Results tripled.

Myth: The best way to motivate the group is to have a contest with a grand prize for the winner.

Despite the American love of competition, contests don't work well. Here's why:

1. An incentive program with one winner and many losers is rarely effective more than once.
2. Employees need to work together as a team. It is counterproductive to pit employees against one another.
3. Contests frequently set unrealistically high goals, a practice that sets up most participants for failure.
4. Contests run too long. A winner usually emerges early, which encourages the rest of the staff to give up.

Myth: Give people a specific numerical goal, and they'll do whatever it takes to get there.

Actually, specific numerical goals can be used as a club to punish people. Here's our advice on measurement.

1. Don't measure people against fixed numerical standards, for example, 95 percent first-run quality. Your minimum standards will, in practice, be interpreted by employees as maximum standards. Also, you may overlook significant improvements that fall short of the goal. I have seldom seen an organization fail if it was improving in all major areas and celebrating those improvements.
2. Don't measure employees against each other. Motivating people shouldn't become a race. If people in your organization hide information from each other and make end-runs

around co-workers, you're overemphasizing competition.

3. Do measure each employee's (or department's) current level of performance against his previous level. This way, everyone can win.

You probably don't have to motivate your superstars. They're usually self-motivated. All you have to do is keep out of the way and be a cheerleader. You *do* have to motivate the rest of your staff. The name of the game is to raise the performance of the entire group.

Myth: Money is the primary motivator.

People constantly ask, "Is money a motivator?" That's the wrong question. The question is, "In whose hands is money a motivator?" Here are the real issues:

1. Can the manager present a cash incentive so it's a motivator? Some managers can. Others can't hand someone a $10,000 bonus without insulting him.
2. Do cash incentives fit the culture and values of your organization?
3. Is the cash incentive only for salespeople? This may reward a small group of employees and punish those who must process the extra paperwork.
4. Do the employees of the organization trust management? If you have trust, financial incentives will work. If you don't, no amount of money will work. If you have a trust problem, forget about a new incentive program. Work on trust first. Improve the human atmosphere and then consider a well-designed incentive program.

In general, complicated bonus or profit-sharing plans affect performance minimally. They take too long to pay out and usually lead to dissension and jealousy.

TESTING MOTIVATION

How well do you understand the basics of motivation?

Complete the test below. Listed are ten things commonly used in America today to motivate people toward better performance. Check the ones you think will work.

1. Yes ☐ No ☐

   Each worker is given a $100 bonus at the end of the year if the accident rate improves.

2. Yes ☐ No ☐

   Employees are given the privilege of choosing their benefits cafeteria style.

3. Yes ☐ No ☐

   Managers and employees agree on a realistic goal for improving productivity. Profit sharing takes place at the end of the month for those who meet the goal.

4. Yes ☐ No ☐

   Employees are given a choice of working hours through flextime.

5. Yes ☐ No ☐

   Based on achievement, employees can choose their own working hours.

6. Yes ☐ No ☐

   An across-the-board salary increase of 4 percent is given.

7. Yes ☐ No ☐

   Each employee not absent or tardy for one week competes in a $100 drawing.

8. Yes ☐ No ☐

   Regular performance reviews take place every six months and carefully measure each person's performance.

9. Yes ☐ No ☐

   Job descriptions list all required duties.

10. Yes ☐ No ☐

   A bonus system allows each employee to receive a share of corporate earnings at the end of the year.

Although it could be argued that any of these things could work in isolated, special circumstances, our firm has thirty years of applied research to indicate that only three motivators in this list will result in improvement: numbers three, five, and seven.

Test Answers:
1. No—The reward is too far removed from the performance.
2. No—It's a giveaway. The employees didn't have to earn it.
3. Yes—This is the pay system of Japan, and it is beginning to be used by U.S. companies.
4. No—Same problem as number two.
5. Yes—The employees have to earn this priviledge, and this system is working in many places.
6. No—This system has been the U.S. system for many years—while worker productivity has declined.
7. Yes—One company's recent investment ($5,200) gave it an annualized return of $700,000 in fewer days taken off.
8. No—There is growing evidence that performance reviews are a waste of time.
9. No—Rewards follow behavior. Nevertheless, a job description is important.
10. No—The reward is too far removed from the work. Only top management is motivated by bonuses.

Let me comment further on a few of these ideas, since they are crucial to motivation. Why won't number one work? Simple. Rank-and-file employees will not work today for a reward they will receive months away. In fact, the six most deadly words in motivation are *at the end of the year.* This is the fatal flaw in most bonus or profit-sharing programs.

Here's a law of human behavior you should memorize:

People behave on a daily basis because of what happens to them on a daily basis.

Number three is the pay system in the Empire of Japan in

almost every company and governmental agency. The only difference in the governmental agencies is that the profit requirement is removed.

If I were a worker at Toyota City today, my salary might be something like $30,000, if yen were converted into dollars. But that wouldn't be my official salary, because everybody has three salaries. My minimum salary might be $18,000. The remaining $12,000 would be divided into twelve monthly increments of $1,000 a month. I would receive that money as a separate check at the end of the month so long as two things were true: (1) the organization is on-track with its goals of quality, productivity, and earnings and (2) my team is on-target with its team goals of quality and productivity. The organization could be doing well, but if my team is missing its goal, we wouldn't get the extra $1,000. We would still get the $1,500 each month, but not the extra $1,000.

Also, if my team is able to figure out how to go beyond the goals and levels we originally set for ourselves, we can receive, in addition, an amount equal to half of our $30,000 base pay, or $15,000. Technically, my salary could be as low as $18,000 or as high as $45,000, depending on how well my team does and how sharp our teamwork and thinking is.

If somebody on my team isn't carrying his share of the load, who takes care of that? The other team members, not management. Probably 70 to 80 percent of the problems with marginal performers American managers spend so much time on would never reach the management level in Japan. Instead, the team would sit down with that person and say, "Look, you are letting us down. You are costing us. It's unacceptable." There is intense peer pressure in Japan to perform at a level of excellence.

A Japanese worker never knows how much money he or she is making. The one thing he does know is that he's going to come to work every day with one thought uppermost in his mind: *How can I contribute the most?* Not, Where can I find a nice place to hide until five o'clock, but, How can I contribute the most? And the second thought uppermost in his mind is, *How can I help my team?* Does that make a difference in the way an organization functions? Let me tell you an astounding story.

I have been close to the automobile industry for a long time. Until a few years ago, when a car rolled off the assembly line in an automobile plant in the U.S., it had been inspected some two hundred times. And after all of that, the car was sent to a place called "the pit," where a team of better-than-average engineers gave it one more fine-tooth-comb inspection. Then it was sent to the loading dock to be shipped, or it was returned to the assembly line, with orange tags hanging all over it specifying things to be redone.

What is interesting is that most plants had to rework approximately seven out of a hundred cars. Mind you, that was after the cars had been inspected two hundred times.

In Japan, where I did my postdoctoral fellowship a number of years ago, they do not inspect cars at all as they are being made. They omit all two hundred of those steps. Instead, when a car is completed, it goes directly to "the pit," where an inspection team descends on it. But rather than having to redo seven out of a hundred cars, they only have to redo six out of one hundred thousand.

If you are running an American automobile plant and you hear this story, the burning question in your mind should be, *Why?* Why is there this difference? The answer lies in the reward system. Recognition in Japan occurs frequently and is team-based. More important, the Japanese reward system creates a tremendous spirit of teamwork.

THE ABCs OF BEHAVIOR

The system I would like to propose in this book is even better than the one in Japan. It is based on a concept developed by a man who spent most of his life teaching at Harvard University, B. F. Skinner. Now when most people study psychology in high school or college, they get a brief exposure to Skinner. That exposure usually deals with his early experiments with pigeons, which weren't terribly interesting, and they never see the towering importance of his mature work in the workplace, where he tested his ideas and theories.

Skinner described human behavior as a matter of ABCs. *A* stands for *activator*. An activator could be anything that starts a chain of human behavior. It causes performance to happen. It could be a job description, instructions, a command, or even a ringing telephone that says, "Pick me up." It could be a vision statement, a mission statement, or stated goals for the organization—any one of a thousand things. We don't lack for activators.

The activator is supposed to be followed by B, or *behavior*. If you want to use a more business-oriented term, it's performance.

Is there a big difference between the activator and the behavior, between what's supposed to be done and what's really done? Yes, because we overlook the most important of the three steps of the chain of human behavior, C, or the *consequences*. We ignore one of Skinner's basic principles: Behavior is a function of its consequences, not of its activators.

I was raised in a home where one parent delivered all the activators and the other parent delivered all the consequences. Mom was great at activators. She would meet me in the morning at nine o'clock and say, "Son, I'm so glad I ran into you. I've been wanting to talk to you about our family. A family is just like a team."

"Hey, Mom, don't give me the team speech. What you want me to do is mow the grass."

"That's right, I want you to mow that grass today."

"Can I have breakfast first, or is this critical?"

At about ten-thirty, she'd say, "You haven't forgotten that grass, have you?"

"No, I haven't forgotten that grass. That grass is one of the most important things in my life because you mention it every hour."

About one-thirty in the afternoon, she'd start getting mad. "You could have mowed the grass all morning while it was nice and cool. Now the neighbors are going to see you out there in the afternoon and will think I'm raising a fool for a son."

About four o'clock, she went into her famous "after-all-I've-done-for-you" talk. But what hadn't changed amid all these activators? Behavior.

Behavior changed radically at 6:00 P.M. That's when Dad got home. I would hear this male voice say, "Thomas Joseph, you get out there and mow that lawn right now."

By the time he said "now," I was down two flights of stairs, had the mower out of the garage, and had cut one swath across the back.

My father never messed around with activators. You got one activator followed immediately by the consequence. So he was always the "changer" of behavior.

I've seen homes where it is just the reverse—where the mother delivered all the consequences—but I guarantee you that whoever delivers the consequences is the one who influences behavior.

Did you ever hear a supervisor say, "If I've told him once, I've told him a thousand times, do it the other way"? Well, if the supervisor has said it a thousand times, the thousand and first time won't do the trick. It is not going to be a watershed event for the employee.

But too often we don't think of that. If the first activator doesn't work, we are likely to send out a second one. If the first memo doesn't make a difference, we send out another memo. If the first meeting doesn't work, we have another meeting. We are forgetting Skinner's lesson: Activators are important but what determines behavior in the long term is consequences.

TAPPING THE INNER SPIRIT

These consequences have to be real, and any changes proposed should tap into the inner spirit of the employees.

I learned this years ago as a young human resources executive at a packing plant. Have you ever been in a packing plant? Everyone should tour one. It would give you a tremendous appreciation for your current job. It's not an assembly plant—it's a disassembly plant. It is also a dangerous place, because you work with a lot of sharp instruments. On top of that, some parts of the plant have to be kept below freezing year-round, so it's not a very pleasant place to work.

It was my duty one night to drive up to this plant with a consultant and hold an all-employee meeting. I said, "Look—here are the facts. You make sixteen to eighteen dollars an hour. Our competition in this state pays six to eight dollars an hour. We have an old plant. Their plant is brand-new. We're losing several million dollars a year, and they're making money. We have three choices. Choice number one: Cut our wages in half. Choice number two: Close the plant—which is what some in the management team want to do. Choice number three: Let's work to make this the most productive plant of its kind in the United States within the limits of the equipment. Which would you like to work on?"

The meeting was supposed to last until nine or ten o'clock. At 3:00 A.M. we were still generating ideas. Six weeks later, we had eighteen improvement projects going—all employee-generated. Soon we had eighty. A year later, the company broke even. The year after that, it made a million dollars. The year after that, it made $3 million and began replacing the equipment. The plant has never missed a day. No one has ever been laid off. The product produced in that plant has become nationally recognized for quality.

I learned two things that night. When faced with consequences, people can change—fast. I also learned that a trove of great ideas exists in the minds of rank-and-file employees. The employees got excited. They were energized. They were having fun. And they generated change.

MOTIVATED EMPLOYEES

Motivated employees always seem to have certain characteristics.

They have some control.

Motivated employees feel they are in control of their work situation. This has been a hard lesson for managers like me, who were trained that the essence of management is to control others. Today we understand that it is sometimes necessary to relinquish control to get results.

They work for leaders who have true humility.

This doesn't mean that good leaders have to devalue or trivialize their own worth or think less of themselves. They will simply think of themselves less. They will focus on the talent and giftedness of their team members. They will always be affirming them. They will share control with others and get excited about their successes.

They work for an organization that has a worthy purpose.

People want to believe that the business or organization they are investing half of their conscious lives in is worth the investment. They want to believe that it produces a product or service of value to others and is a positive force in the world. They want to work for an organization that invests energy and time crafting and communicating its mission. There is nothing more enjoyable than to spend your life doing work you enjoy, with colleagues you respect, in an organization worth giving your life for.

They have some problems.

Believe it or not, the most fulfilled people I've known in business always have major problems they are working on. They love the challenge of unraveling a complex problem and putting a solution into place.

They are learning.

Satisfied members of a corporate family are people who are growing, changing, and developing. They are lifelong learners who create organizations where people learn. Training takes place in the classroom, but learning takes place in the organization itself.

One of my earliest mentors in the business world was a man named Harold Hamil. Harold had been a newspaper editor prior to heading the public relations and administrative services area of a huge agribusiness cooperative. He had a keen mind and a great zest for learning and life. He hated the status quo. He hated mediocrity. He reminded me that great speeches and articles are not so much written as they are rewritten and rewritten. He was a fascinating person to be around. He modeled for me the role of a lifelong learner. It was because of him that I went on to earn two degrees while holding responsible full-time positions.

They work with leaders who have emotional and spiritual depth.

Happy, healthy, fulfilled leaders and employees always have a spiritual dimension to their lives. I make no apology for this statement. I make it almost every time I address a business convention or a leadership workshop. I've been observing business leaders for nearly forty years, and I've yet to meet one who succeeded in building a long-term life of balanced growth and success who did not have a spiritual dimension to his or her life.

In a recent interview, Ken Blanchard told of his own growing awareness of this. He explained that he had always emphasized self-esteem in his leadership seminars. He began to realize, however, that people who do not have a high view of their own worth and value cannot play the roles of team leadership.

> I began to wonder if effective leadership doesn't begin on the inside and move out. After all, only people who genuinely like themselves can build the self-esteem of others without feeling that it takes something away from themselves. My concern with self-esteem coincided with my own renewed spiritual interest. In confronting my own spirituality, I began to sense that a spiritual awakening is perhaps the quickest and most powerful way to significantly enhance self-esteem and make ourselves more loving.
>
> I know I am taking a risk with some of you when I mention God, but I think we can get ourselves into trouble if we believe there is nothing more powerful, knowledgeable and loving than ourselves.
>
> My wife, Margie, and I were leading a seminar on personal excellence last fall at Yosemite Park. One of the participants objected to my references to a higher power. Later in the weekend, we took people to work on their mission statements at Glacier Point, a breathtaking summit 3,000 feet above the valley floor. I noticed my unbelieving friend standing at the edge, looking thoughtfully at the gorgeous spectacle. I walked over to him, and the two of us stood there for a few moments taking it in. I said, "It's a beautiful accident, isn't it?" We both laughed.[2]

The leader of the future will be the one who can tap into the wellspring of selfless love and the deep need for connectedness that is within all people.

Does this seem too idealistic for a business manager? The chairman of Matushita Electric was recently asked to state what he believed to be his highest priority as chief executive of a vast corporation. This was his response:

> To model love. I am the soul of this company. It is through me that our organization's values pass.[3]

REFERENCES

1. Steven R. Covey, "What's Holding Back Quality? Total Trust," *Quality Digest*, March 1995, 21.
2. Ken Blanchard, "The Spiritual Workplace," *Quality Digest*, March 1995, 18.
3. Quoted in Norman Vincent Peale and Kenneth H. Blanchard, *The Power of Ethical Management* (New York: Fawcett Crest, 1988), 89.

3

THE MANAGER
◼
Deepening the Inner Spirit

For the last several decades I have been involved in the improvement of the quality of human performance in the workplace. My firm specializes in Total Quality Management, and we have assisted in installing such programs in more than one hundred major corporations.

Frequently we begin such programs by interviewing a large number of key management and nonmanagement persons to get their perspective on the organization. Early in this process, someone usually confides to me in hushed tones, "Tom, I can't put my finger on it, but there is just something missing from this place."

I have come to believe that the mysterious missing element is meaning—a sense of connectedness between what employees do and who they are. This has given me a renewed interest in what I can only refer to as spirituality in the workplace. A closely related interest is the spiritual depth and maturity of management.

When business managers have a strong spiritual faith, that faith lifts them beyond themselves and their narrower interests. They have greater respect for themselves. They can play many roles, but they are not their roles. They can and do employ good management techniques, but they do not become their techniques. They have respect for their associates and see them as persons first and employees second. There is a great hunger in America for this new type of spiritually mature manager.

How else do you explain the enormous popularity of Steven Covey's books *Principle-Centered Leadership, The Seven Habits of Highly Successful People,* and *First Things First: A Principle-Centered Approach to Time and Life Management*? These books resonate in the business community because we are sick of books on manipulative techniques and how to survive office politics. Covey was the first major writer in a long while to emphasize that the first task of a leader is not to *do* something, but to *be* something.

Psychologist and management consultant O. A. Ohmann states: "Our people have lost faith in the basic values of our economic society. . . . We need a spiritual rebirth in industrial leadership. . . . Can it be that our god of production has feet of clay? Does industry need a new religion—or at least a better one than it has had?"[1]

Parker Palmer says: "There is an illness in our culture: it arises from our rigid separation of the visible world from the powers that undergird and animate it. With that separation we diminish life, capping off its sources of healing, hope, and wholeness."[2]

You see the same "something is missing" feeling in society as a whole. It is not surprising that one of the top-selling books today is Thomas Moore's *Care of the Soul,* which shows how we can nourish the inner spirit in the small everyday events of life.[3] M. Scott Peck's *The Road Less Traveled,* which highlights how psychotherapy may help us connect to our inner spirituality, has been on best-seller lists for more than five hundred weeks.[4] Both books are guides for finding spiritual meaning in life and work.

This emphasis is more important for business than ever before. Why? Because the corporation has become our new community. I don't say this with great joy. A better source of community, connectedness, and spiritual nourishment would be the family. But the family is in shambles. It is fractured and splintered, and children are rarely raised by both their original parents. The extended family of grandparents and relatives live in faraway cities.

Nor are neighborhoods any longer communities. Once when my wife and I moved into a new home, we decided to get acquainted by having a block party. We invited everyone on both sides of the block. We assumed we would be the strangers in a community of friends but were astonished to find that our neighbors didn't know each other. We spent the evening introducing them to one another.

This vacuum of community has placed enormous stress on the corporation. People expect to discover and fulfill the meaning of their lives through work. Employees also bring an enormous array of personal problems to work and expect somehow, somewhere, to find help. For many, the corporation has become their most important community.

Leaders shape the vision, values, and ethics of an organization, so it is important for us to have leaders who can bring people together and create a community built on shared vision. Such leaders, says Stanford management professor Harold Leavitt, will by their "vision, values, and determination add soul to the organization."[5] Warren Bennis and Burt Nanus, in their landmark book, *Leaders,* say that "by focusing attention on a vision, the leader operates on the emotional and spiritual resources of the organization, on its values, commitment, and aspirations."[6]

Great organizations have a corporate soul, or spirit. It is not a shallow thing, and they know how to communicate it. Robert Lynn, former vice president for the Lilly Endowment, describes the importance of this approach:

> What happens at the deeper levels, the "subsoil" of institutional life, is . . . more significant than any skill training for a particular position. The strength and vitality of an institution arise from the unseen depths. The best educational programs will help leaders explore the institution's subsoil.[7]

Peter Drucker believes that organizations begin to die when they lose their spiritual vision. This is true, for example, of colleges. The colleges most alive and thriving today, he says, are conservative Christian colleges, not the large, multipurpose universities.

If you look for the institution that has done the best marketing job, it's the fundamentalist college. Precisely because it is a boutique, it doesn't try to do anything but a very narrow specialty. . . . But the comprehensive universities that did so well in the fifties and sixties are beginning to, I would say, lose character in the public mind. That explains why the good liberal arts college, which we all thought was going to be in severe trouble fifteen years ago when student populations began to go down, is doing so very well. . . . The kid can get his or her arms around it, and it has a personality, whereas the University of Minnesota or UCLA are very hard to describe.[8]

A surprising number of senior executives at Fortune 500 companies are actively religious. In a recent survey of a hundred business executives, 65 percent said they worshiped at churches or synagogues on a regular basis. This compares to a national average of 40 percent for all Americans.

The worship experience of today's executives is quite different from that of several decades ago when one went to church to see and be seen. A summary of the survey described today's business leaders as "under stress and seeking meaning, inspiration, and guidance for their lives."[9]

There are also major companies run by leaders who actively espouse spiritual values in the hopes that they will guide company behavior. The head of Mary Kay Cosmetics attributes her company's success directly to God:

We succeeded with a foundation built upon the Golden Rule and a philosophy of God first, family second, and career third, giving women a chance to keep their lives in the proper perspective.

ServiceMaster, a more than $1 billion company that manages services ranging from food preparation to housekeeping to equipment maintenance for institutions, even has a spiritual emphasis that is evident in its name, which can be expanded to "Service to the Master." The company's ultimate goal is "to honor God in all we do."[10]

One leading executive stated that he believed his gifts and skills were entrusted to his stewardship for "maximum self-development and useful service to one's fellows in the hope that one may live a rich life and be a credit to his Creator. . . . It is against this frame of reference that the decisions of the moment easily fall into proper perspective."[11]

The spiritually connected manager has many advantages.

His base of power is not in the position.

He understands that it's not all up to him. He knows that, in the midst of seeming chaos, a sovereign God is working for good and will bring all things to a perfect completion.

> People who feel powerless, whether they are managers or those being managed, tend to hoard whatever shreds of power they have. Powerless managers tend to adopt petty and dictatorial management styles. They create organizational systems where political skills are essential and passing the buck is the favorite way of handling problems.[12]

I once worked with an organization where power was a zero-sum game. For every winner there had to be a loser. If one executive was up, another had to be down. People even went to discussion meetings with a competitive win-lose mind-set. We sat around after meetings and discussed who won and who lost. If a problem arose, the focus was on fixing blame, not on fixing the problem. People hid information from each other and constantly made end runs around one another. It was a chilling atmosphere. It killed my spirit. The firm had lost its spiritual soul.

You can always tell when you're in a company managed by an insecure, power-retaining manager. Everyone talks about The Boss. "He said this." "She did that." "He thinks this way." Nothing can happen unless The Boss "blesses" it.

In well-managed organizations, power is shared, given away to other talented members of the team. It may take a while to figure out who is the boss. One writer puts it this way:

> A leader is best when people barely know that he or she exists.
>
> Not so good when people obey and acclaim him.
>
> Worse when they despise him.

> If you fail to honor people, they fail to honor you; but of a good leader, who talks little, when his work is done, his aim fulfilled, they all say, "We did this ourselves."[13]

I once knew an executive who yelled and screamed at his employees and publicly attacked and humiliated his staff. It was not enough to disagree with an associate. He had to destroy him. Later, he would be remorseful and offer long apologies. He sent gifts and flowers to atone. What he could not see was that the damage could not be undone. Once people are punished for trying to be creative and collaborative, they learn the lesson well. They quit contributing. They defer to the boss—and look for other employment opportunities. His apologies were irrelevant.

You can tell such organizations by their vocabulary: over/under, top/bottom, superiors/subordinates, upper level/lower level. They spend vast amounts of time drawing stove-pipe organizational charts to keep everyone in place. Such companies do not grow and learn.

Management thinker Peter Senge, in his book on organizations, *The Fifth Discipline*, writes:

> Team learning starts with "dialogue," the capacity of members of a team to suspend assumptions and enter into a genuine "thinking together." To the Greeks dialogos meant a free-flowing of meaning through a group, allowing the group to discover insights not attainable individually.[14]

Harrison Owen, an Episcopal minister, believes that our obsession with structure causes us to build it first and then try to squeeze the spirit in. "Creating structure before attending to spirit," he says, "is like buying a pair of shoes without measuring your feet."[15]

The irony is that a manager in a rigid hierarchical system gets out of touch. It's almost comical to witness. The very person who wants to run everything ends up not knowing anything about what's going on under his nose. He is sealed off from honest, corrective feedback. Such managers complain that others are not stepping up and assuming their responsibility, yet they themselves are the reason that is happening.

Spiritually connected managers have the greatest of all management gifts—perspective and judgment.

Blanchard and Peale describe perspective as "the capacity to see what is really important in any given situation."[16] Today we have tons of data but little "profound knowledge," as Deming often described it. The habit of reflection is critical to acquiring a sense of perspective. And reflection is not possible unless some time each day is devoted to silence—a resource that has been recommended by wise men of all time and from all cultures, and yet one that remains mostly untapped.

Peter Kreeft says: "If I were a doctor and I could prescribe just one remedy for all the ills of the modern world, I would prescribe silence. For even if the word of God were proclaimed in the modern world, no one would hear it, because of the panoply of noise."[17]

Spiritual managers have deep respect for their associates. They were natural team builders before team building became a buzzword.

If we successfully come to terms with our inner spiritual reality, we will appreciate that ours is not the only act in town. Not only are there other acts in town, but some are much better than ours.

The Bible provides excellent case studies of leaders. King Rehoboam chose to ignore God's approach to management and tried to "lord it over" his people. Rehoboam asked the elder statesmen how he should lead the nation. They replied, "If today you will be a servant to these people and serve them and give them a favorable answer, they will always be your servants" (1 Kings 12:7). But King Rehoboam ignored their advice and used his power and authority to manipulate, control, and exploit. As a result, the nation rebelled against him, and he lost the majority of his people.

Myron Rush believes that Jesus was the greatest example of a servant leader.

Jesus Christ knew this principle well. He came to give His life to and for people. That was His major goal. And He spent a great deal of time challenging and training people to get involved in "a piece of the action." For example, He said to Simon Peter and his brother Andrew, "Come, follow me, and I will make you fishers of men" (Matt. 4:19).

The disciples recognized the value, importance, and potential of the job Jesus was offering them. They realized here was a Leader willing to use their abilities and creativity to do the same job He was doing. Their reaction to this type of offer is recorded in the next verse: "At once they left their nets and followed him" (v. 20).

However, many leaders tell their people, "Follow me and you can have all of the jobs I don't want." Jesus not only recognized the unlimited potential and value of human creativity, He offered His followers training and opportunity to put their ability to work in a worthwhile cause. This is the mark of an excellent leader and manager of human resources.[18]

Jesus stated His own leadership philosophy clearly:

> Among the heathen, kings are tyrants and each minor official lords it over those beneath him. But among you it is quite different. Anyone wanting to be a leader among you must be your servant. And if you want to be right at the top, you must serve like a slave. Your attitude must be like my own, for I, the Messiah, did not come to be served, but to serve. (Matthew 20:25–28 TLB)

An effective leader once told him, Rush says, "If you train a man, he will become what you are, but if you serve him, the sky is the limit as to what he can become."[19]

Spiritually secure leaders deal with mistakes in a creative way. They don't love mistakes, but they see the person behind the mistake.

Spiritually secure leaders use mistakes as opportunities for growth. "One of the things . . . we need to understand better in organizational life," Max DePree says, "is the role of grace. Mistakes are not terminal. Mistakes are part of education with, of course, some exceptions. When we challenge people on the high side, the odds are much better that we're going to get both better performance and more development of the person."[20]

Warren Bennis and Burt Nanus believe that leaders have a special attitude toward failure:

> For a lot of people, the word "failure" carries with it a finality, the absence of movement characteristic of a dead thing, to which the automatic human reaction is helpless discouragement. But for the successful leader, failure is a beginning, the springboard of hope.[21]

Spiritual managers know that their own journey toward maturity has been filled with mistakes. M. Scott Peck's reflections on grace describe the problem that we must face as we wrestle with spiritual development:

> We do not come to grace, grace comes to us. Try as hard as we might to obtain grace, it may yet elude us. We may seek it not, yet it will find us. Consciously we may avidly desire the spiritual life but then discover all manner of stumbling blocks in our way. Or we may have seemingly little taste for spiritual life and yet find ourselves vigorously called to it in spite of ourselves. While on one level, we do choose whether or not to heed the call of grace, on another it seems clear that God is the one who does the choosing. The common experience of those who have achieved a state of grace . . . is one of amazement at their condition. They do not feel they have earned it.[22]

Spiritually secure leaders are confident and project a positive vision for the future.

Possibly the nicest compliment I ever received from a colleague in a difficult management situation was her statement, "Tom, the one thing you brought into our firm was hope. You calmed us down and gave us the feeling that we could overcome any problem." I've always treasured that bit of positive reinforcement.

Insecure leaders project fear. That does not mean we won't have fears. We will have fears aplenty. But we don't have to become our fears or lead from fear. We don't have to project our fears on others, but rather we can lead from an inner place of trust and hope.

I used to wonder why Jesus began so many of His conversations with His disciples by saying, "Do not be afraid." Then I realized He did so because He was training leaders—imperfect, flawed leaders—who would found the world's largest, longest enduring, and most successful organization, the church.

He was teaching them as He has taught me that who I am does not depend on what I do. My central identity is not in titles or degrees or functions. It depends on the fact that I am a child of God, valued and treasured for who I am. When a leader knows that, the office, the sales territory, and the plant will be a different place.

REFERENCES

1. O. A. Ohmann, "Skyhooks," in *Ethics in Practice: Managing the Moral Corporation*, ed. K. P. Andrews (Boston: Harvard Business School Press, 1989), 59.

2. Parker J. Palmer, *To Know As We Are Known: A Spirituality of Education* (San Francisco: Harper, 1983), 72.

3. Thomas Moore, *Care of the Soul: A guide for Cultivating Depth and Sacredness in Everyday Life* (San Francisco: HarperCollins, 1993).

4. M. Scott Peck, *The Road Less Traveled: A New Psychology of Love, Traditional Values and Spiritual Growth* (New York: Touchstone, 1978).

5. Harold J. Leavitt, *Corporate Pathfinders* (Homewood, Ill.: Dow Jones-Irwin, 1986), 95.

6. Warren G. Bennis and Burt Nanus, *Leaders: Their Strategies for Taking Charge* (New York: HarperCollins, 1985), 92.

7. Robert Lynn, "Penetrating the Mystery of Leadership Through Depth Education," *The 1984 Lilly Endowment Annual Report* (Indianapolis, Ind.: Lilly Endowment, 1984), 8.

8. Peter F. Drucker, *Managing the Non-Profit Organization* (New York: HarperCollins, 1992), 80.

9. "God Gets Down to Business," *Across the Board* (The Conference Board) 14, no. 5 (May 1988), 11–12.

10. E. C. Burg, "Profiting with Help from Above," *Fortune* (27 April 1987), 38.

11. Ohmann, "Skyhooks," 66–67.

12. Jay A. Conger, *Spirit at Work* (San Francisco: Jossey-Boss, 1994), 77.

13. Ibid., 185.

14. Peter Senge, *The Fifth Discipline: Mastering the Five Practices of the Learning Organization* (New York: Doubleday, 1990), 10.

15. Harrison Owen, *Leadership Is* (Potomac, Md.: Abbot, 1980), 85.

16. Norman Vincent Peale and Kenneth H. Blanchard, *The Power of Ethical Management* (New York: Fawcett Crest, 1988), 69.

17. Peter Kreeft, *Making Choices: Practical Wisdom for Everyday Moral Decisions* (Ann Arbor, Mich.: Servant, 1990), 168.

18. Myron D. Rush, *Management: A Biblical Approach* (Wheaton, Ill., Scripture Press, Victor Books, 1983), 28.

19. Ibid., 13–14.

20. Max DePree, in Peter F. Drucker, *Managing the Non-Profit Organization*, 42.

21. Warren Bennis and Bert Nanus, *Leaders*, 69.

22. M. Scott Peck, *The Road Less Traveled*, 307.

4

THE SYSTEM

◼

Releasing the Inner Spirit

The famed New York Yankee manager Casey Stengel used to say that the real art of management was to keep the five players who want to kill you away from the four who are undecided!

In my early business career I was trained in the Casey Stengel School of Management. My colleagues and I talked about the PODCCs of management—*plan, organize, direct, coordinate,* and *control*—and we assumed that the people doing these things should be us, the ones at the top of the pyramid. We didn't consider the possibility that a wealth of ideas could be introduced into an organization by people throughout the pyramid.

This top-down authoritarian school of management leads to one of modern life's worst nightmares—the bureaucracy, that elaborate, complex system designed to control others rather than to accomplish a needed result. It kills the human spirit.

Recently the Associated Press carried the story of an appalling incident that demonstrated the weaknesses of a bureaucracy. A Washington, D.C., boy had been missing—and feared kidnapped—when

> a dozen District of Columbia halfway house residents discovered [him] and his alleged captor wrapped in a blanket in a wooded

area about eight blocks from the boy's southeast Washington home.

The boy was naked and apparently had not eaten in the two days since he was abducted on Thursday while walking to his aunt's house, police said. . . .

Rahim Jenkins, a halfway house employee who helped organize the search, said that when they approached the pink blanket on the wooded hillside on Saturday, "that baby jumped out and said, 'Please don't leave me, help me.'"[1]

Why was the boy was found by the halfway house residents and not the police? The police had refused to "launch an immediate all-out search" because the child "did not meet the criteria for a critical missing person."[2] So the mother called the halfway house.

We see the same problem in our national welfare system. What was intended to be a safety net has become a hammock people cannot get out of. When people try to lift themselves up, the bureaucracy punishes them, as this story illustrates:

NEW HAVEN, May 13, 1992. Working part-time at a community center, Sandra Rosado saved $4,900 to go to college and escape the web of welfare that all her family had known since they moved here 12 years ago.

But her thrift and industry have led to a bureaucratic nightmare for Miss Rosado and her family. First, state officials, who discovered her savings account, told her mother to spend the money so the family could remain eligible for the Aid to Families with Dependent Children program. Then Federal authorities ordered the mother to repay $9,342 in benefits she received while her daughter's money was in the bank.[3]

In the best-selling book *The Death of Common Sense*, Philip K. Howard gives scores of examples of laws and regulations that keep organizations from fulfilling their purpose. Perhaps his most stunning example is one concerning Mother Teresa.

In the winter of 1988, nuns of the Missionaries of Charity were walking through the snow in the South Bronx in their saris and sandals to look for an abandoned building that they might convert into a homeless shelter. Mother Teresa, the Nobel Prize winner and head of the order, had agreed on the plan with Mayor Ed

Koch after visiting him in the hospital several years earlier. The nuns came to two fire-gutted buildings on 148th Street and, finding a Madonna among the rubble, thought that perhaps providence itself had ordained the mission. New York City offered the abandoned buildings at one dollar each, and the Missionaries of Charity set aside $500,000 for the reconstruction. The nuns developed a plan to provide temporary care for sixty-four homeless men in a communal setting that included a dining room and kitchen on the first floor, a lounge on the second floor, and small dormitory rooms on the third and fourth floors. The only unusual thing about the plan was that Missionaries of Charity, in addition to their vow of poverty, avoid the routine use of modern conveniences. There would be no dishwashers or other appliances; laundry would be done by hand. For New York City, the proposed homeless facility would be (literally) a godsend.

Although the city owned the buildings, no official had the authority to transfer them except through an extensive bureaucratic process. For a year and a half the nuns, wanting only to live a life of ascetic service, found themselves instead traveling in their sandals from hearing room to hearing room, presenting the details of the project and then discussing the details again at two higher levels of city government. In September 1989 the city finally approved the plan and the Missionaries of Charity began repairing the fire damage.

Providence, however, was no match for law. New York's building code, they were told after almost two years, requires an elevator in every new or renovated multiple-story building. The Missionaries of Charity explained that because of their beliefs they would never use the elevator, which also would add upward of $100,000 to the cost. The nuns were told the law could not be waived even if an elevator didn't make sense.

Mother Teresa gave up. She didn't want to devote that much extra money to something that wouldn't really help the poor: According to her representative, "The Sisters felt they could use the money much more usefully for soup and sandwiches." In a polite letter to the city expressing their regrets, the Missionaries of Charity noted that the episode "served to educate us about the law and its many complexities."[4]

WHY COMMUNITY-BASED ORGANIZATIONS WORK

The tragedy of this story is that no one really wanted this to happen. Doubtless, many individuals tried to find a way around the building code. People in the governmental bureaucracy—whether local, state, or federal—are not heartless, uncaring people. They are good people tangled up in a complex system of well-intentioned regulations and red tape.

Similarly, reforming welfare doesn't mean creating a heartless, unfeeling, "sink or swim" policy. It means that the welfare bureaucracy we now have does not deliver the care people really need. In my own community, the outstanding caregivers are the Salvation Army, City Union Mission, Catholic Charities, Lutheran Social Services, the Lighthouse Center for Pregnant Teenagers, Habitat for Humanity, and dozens of centers for the homeless and hungry operated by individual churches. All of these agencies are privately funded and privately managed.

David Osborne and Ted Gaebler cite several reasons why community-based, nonbureaucratic organizations are better at meeting human needs:

1. Communities have more commitment to their members than service delivery systems have to their clients.
2. Communities understand their problems better than service professionals.
3. Professionals and bureaucracies deliver services; communities solve problems.
4. Institutions and professionals offer service; communities offer care.
5. Communities are more flexible and creative than large service providers.
6. Private community-based organizations are less expensive than service professionals.
7. Communities enforce standards of behavior more effectively than bureaucracies.
8. Communities focus on capacities; service systems focus on deficiencies.[5]

REENGINEERING SUCCESS STORIES

Bureaucracy is not something that appears only in public

agencies. It appears in the business world as well. When I'm working with a group of managers or employees in a corporation, I like to ask, "If this were your own company, if you were the owner, would you run it the way it's being run today?" Almost invariably the answer is "Of course not!"

Most employees are keenly aware of the waste and inefficiency in the organizations they work for. When given the opportunity, they can redesign those companies in far more effective ways.

In *Reengineering the Corporation*, Michael Hammer and James Champy give many examples of companies that have redesigned themselves.[6] One is the IBM Credit Corporation, the unit of IBM that approves all the loans for small businesses to buy the company's equipment.

Ten years ago, the Credit Corporation had fourteen people working on this process. The first step was to log in the request for credit. One department did that. Then the application went to the credit department. It ran a credit check. Then the application was taken to the business practices department, where the terms of the loan went through a separate computer system. After that, the application went to still another unit, the pricing department, where a pricer determined the interest rate to be applied to the loan. When the application had made this safari through the various departments, it finally went to the clerical department, where the approval was typed up and sent to the customer. The process took one week to complete. That was ten years ago at IBM.

You don't have to be an organizational genius to see tremendous problems with a procedure like that. So IBM created a team to see if something better could be done. One of the first things the team did was to walk a sample loan application through the process to see how long each of the steps really took. They went to each desk and asked the person there to set aside everything else he was working on and process that one test loan. Then they took the application to the next desk and did the same thing. How long do you think it actually, physically took to process the loan? Ninety minutes.

When the team saw how little time it took to complete the loan approval, they reengineered the process. They converted the staff members from specialists to generalists, people who could do all five, six, or seven major steps in the function. The company kept a few specialists who supported the generalists. Then the company integrated its software. (Why a company such as IBM had not done that yet is baffling.)

Today, twelve people work in the Credit Corporation. The average time it takes to process a loan is four hours. Here's the incredible part. Today, the Credit Corporation does one hundred times the volume it did ten years ago. Every organization that intends to survive into the twenty-first century will have to undergo a similar process.

We just finished working with a mortgage banking company. Now if you've ever waited for a house loan to be approved, you know that it frequently takes a month. Fifteen days is minimum, thirty days is average, and forty-five days is not unheard of if there are any problems. The banking company created a team to analyze this process. The team studied it from every conceivable angle. They found that, over the years, every time a special case had come up, a whole new approval procedure had been created to deal with it. So, as they put it, 80 percent of their loans were flowing through a crooked pipe when they could have been flowing through a straight pipe.

They reengineered the process. Today, what once took a minimum of fifteen days to accomplish, and an average of thirty, has been reduced to five days or less. For an organization that processes thousands of loans a month, that is what Hammer and Champy would call a quantum leap forward. It's not just tweaking some little thing. It's really getting back to the basics.

The numbers from reengineering projects are nearly incredible. Here are just a few results:

- Corning has reduced error rates in some of their plants from 1,800 parts per million to 9 or less.
- General Electric used to take three weeks after an order to deliver a custom-made industrial circuit breaker box. Now it takes three days.
- AT&T used to need two years to design a new phone. Now it can do the job in one month.

- Motorola used to turn out electronic pagers three weeks after the factory got the order. Now it takes two hours.
- Reengineered manufacturing plants have typically boosted productivity by 30 to 50 percent (often without layoffs).

Speed is catching on fast. The fifty major U.S. companies all report that time-based strategies are now top priorities for them. Why? Because speed kills the competition. If you come up against a faster competitor and you're not prepared, you're history.

We assisted with a project in an Internal Revenue Service office several years ago. This particular office was almost entirely devoted to collecting fraudulent, overdue accounts. It was not the normal IRS center. Here again, the office created a team to look at the process. To make a long story short, prior to reengineering, the average team collected some $3 million a month; today the average team collects some $7 million a week. It has been estimated that if, for the next decade, the IRS could actually collect all the taxes owed, we could wipe out the national debt. The experience of this one office could have remarkable ramifications if it were applied to the IRS as a whole.

PRIDE TEAMS

A utility customer in Clinton, Missouri, approached a Utili-Corp field crew while it was making some repairs. The customer wanted a new vapor light installed. He assumed it would take several weeks, but instead, a crew member immediately took the order, filled out the paperwork, and installed the light on the spot. The customer was astonished.

This would not have happened in previous years. Why was it happening now? It was only one of hundreds of improvements introduced into the business in the last two years by more than sixty cross-functional employee teams called PRIDE teams.

Here are just a few of the achievements of these teams:

- Reduced delinquent accounts by 15 percent

- Reduced paperwork requirements for field crews by 30 percent
- Improved the safety record by 70 percent
- Found ways to save more than $5 million in headquarters' processes
- Improved the customer satisfaction rating to eight points higher than the national average for utilities
- Reduced labor grievances by 77 percent

These teams are a living fulfillment of the UtiliCorp Statement of Values, which says, in part:

> We will give responsibility and authority to make decisions to the person with the most firsthand knowledge of the situation. We will recognize and respect each others' abilities and skills, building self-esteem and encouraging others to perform at their highest level. We will eliminate bureaucratizing barriers to achieve simplicity, efficiency, and sound, speedy decision making.[7]

THE ORGANIZATION OF THE FUTURE

What will the organization of the future look like?

- It will function with fewer levels in every department.
- Performance-based incentives for teams will become a key component of compensation.
- It will be leaner. It will be more responsive, more results-oriented. It will make work processes simpler.
- The structure will encourage the entrepreneurial spirit— greater ownership and accountability, not only for the customer's business but for one's own accomplishments.
- It will have fewer, better people, working harder, in the right structure, and properly "incentivized" to be significantly more productive.

This is the organization Toffler envisioned at the beginning of the 1980s.

Third Wave organizations have flatter hierarchies. They are less top-heavy. They consist of small components linked together in temporary configurations. Each of these components has its own relationship with the outside world, its own foreign policy, so to speak, which it maintains without having to go through the center.[8]

WHAT REENGINEERING IS NOT

It is not a new form of industrial engineering.

Industrial engineering focuses on task analysis, job design, efficiency, and man-hours required per job. It also concentrates on the technological aspects of machine design and work layout. When it addresses human issues at all, it is usually limited in scope to ergonomic design, not to the larger systems design issues of how people actually work together and use technology.

Industrial engineers make a valuable contribution to productivity improvement by concentrating on improvement of existing work processes and procedures. Unfortunately, their work has often resulted in work force reductions and layoffs. I've known consultants who specialize in manpower studies and the traditional industrial engineering approach who have actually had their cars destroyed or their personal safety threatened in plants and offices because their work is so hated.

It is not simply downsizing the workforce.

Unfortunately, this is the primary focus of the Federal Government's "Reinventing" campaign. It is widely touted that the federal system is trimming 100,000 jobs per year and plans to increase this number. Very little is ever said, however, about improving services.

Leaving bureaucratic systems in place while reducing the number of bureaucrats to handle them just creates an even more sluggish, unresponsive system. The citizen (customer) is not better served. Many corporations also make this mistake. In fact the traditional approach to organizational improvement has followed this model:

The result of this approach:

1. We have not fundamentally changed the way we do work.
2. The work load stays the same. Resources decline.
3. The most talented people leave.
4. Morale declines.
5. Eventually some work processes get reengineered, but at enormous human cost.

It is not simply restructuring the management team or reorganizing the company.

Redrawing the boxes on the organizational chart or combining functions in different administrations is not reengineering, even though companies love to do this. Gifford and Elizabeth Pinchot, in *The End of Bureaucracy and the Rise of the Intelligent Organization*, remind us of the danger of constant reorganization by citing this entry from the Journal of Petronius:

We trained hard . . . but it seemed that every time we were beginning to form up into teams, we would be reorganized. I was to
learn later in life that we tend to meet any situation by reorganiz-
ing; and a wonderful method it can be for creating the illusion of
progress while producing confusion, inefficiency, and demoral-
ization.[9]

It is not slow, evolutionary change.

Reengineering involves a quantum leap, not incremental
change. This point is frequently missed by managers, because
moving incrementally "provides a safety net by not changing too
much," as Drew Lathin points out in *The Journal for Quality and
Participation*. The danger in following such an approach is that

> for many American organizations it is just not fast enough. Foreign
> competition is also improving continuously. Continuous improve-
> ment is a realistic strategy for change only when an organization is
> highly competitive and the improvements required of them are in
> the tens of percent, not hundreds. When a company finds itself far
> behind the competition a quantum leap strategy is the only way to
> close the gap, not evolutionary continuous improvement.[10]

It is not simply creating teams and turning them loose to solve problems.

I've seen teams do exciting things, but only when they are
part of an organization-wide commitment that is comprehensive, systemic, and in-depth in terms of work processes. Drew
Lathin comments on the history of too many teams:

> Once the easy-to-solve problems had been solved, the systemic
> issues like work process, team structure, inappropriate reward
> systems, bureaucratic practices, and workers' limited skill sets
> that impeded organizational performance still remained to be
> transformed. Most problem-solving teams did not receive a man-
> date to tackle these systemic problems. . . . Focusing only on the
> team ignores the larger work system in which it exists. The result
> of this narrow focus has been that numerous systems incon-
> gruities are created between the teams and their larger environ-
> ment. Questions concerning structure, reward systems, informa-
> tion systems, supervisors' roles, job classifications, and so on,
> need to be addressed and the incongruities resolved.[11]

One more thing reengineering is not—it is not easy!

WHAT IS REENGINEERING?

Michael Hammer and James Champy, in their classic book, *Reengineering the Corporation,* describe reengineering as

> the fundamental rethinking and radical redesign of business processes to achieve dramatic improvements in critical, contemporary measures of performance, such as cost, quality, service, and speed.[12]

Later the authors offer an even simpler two-word definition: starting over.

> Reengineering is about beginning again with a clean sheet of paper. It is about rejecting the conventional wisdom and received assumptions of the past. Reengineering is about inventing new approaches to process structure that bear little or no resemblance to those of previous eras.[13]

When reengineering really works, it has certain characteristics.

- A clear focus on improving service to the customer, not simply reducing costs or making things easier for the organization.
- A willingness to question everything. We have to ask the "why" question repeatedly. Why do we do it this way? Why did we begin doing it this way? Why do we think this is the best way?
- The courage to give up turf, titles, position, perks, and power; the willingness to see sacred cows slaughtered, pet projects abandoned, and "protected persons" forced to make it on their own.
- The willingness to overhaul the reward system and the way people get promoted. We can't continue preaching "team, team, team" and then reward people as individuals. We

can't continue to teach "quality" in the corporate class-room and then reward quantity at the manufacturing plant. Our walk must match our talk.

- We must be willing to make extensive changes in the organizational structure, including its senior officers. This is especially true if the organization is facing a crisis. It is doubtful that an organization can get out of trouble by retaining the entire leadership team that got it into trouble.
- The plans for the future must be an integrated whole. The Reengineering Plan, the Quality Plan, the Strategic Plan must all be the same plan arrived at through the same comprehensive process.

For an organization to make a quantum leap forward, a process of simultaneous reengineering must be put into place. This process must deal with:

- strategic direction
- work processes
- organizational structure
- organizational culture
- information flow
- measurement in alignment with strategic direction
- rewards and recognition

The key word here is *simultaneous*. All of these changes have to move forward at the same time daily operations continue and customers' needs are met through the current structure.

As I said before, it's not easy.

REFERENCES

1. "Ex-convicts Find Abducted Boy in Woods," *The Kansas City Star*, 3 October 1994. From The Associated Press–Washington, D.C.
2. Ibid.
3. Constance L. Hays, "Girl's Plan to Save for College Runs Afoul of Welfare Rules," *New York Times*, 15 May 1992.
4. Philip K. Howard, *The Death of Common Sense* (New York: Random, 1994), 3–5.

5. David Osborne and Ted Gaebler, *Reinventing Government: How the Entrepreneurial Spirit Is Transforming the Public Sector* (Reading, Mass.: Addison-Wesley, 1992), 65–70.

6. Michael Hammer and James Champy, *Reengineering the Corporation: A Manifesto for Business Revolution* (New York: Harper Business, 1993), 32.

7. UtiliCorp Statement of Mission and Corporate Values.

8. Alvin Toffler, *The Third Wave* (New York: Morrow, 1980), 38.

9. Gifford Pinchot and Elizabeth Pinchot, *The End of Bureaucracy and the Rise of the Intelligent Organization* (San Francisco: Berrett-Koehler, 1993), 200.

10. Drew Lathin, "In the Midst of the Reengineering Forest," *The Journal for Quality and Participation*, January-February 1995, 59.

11. Ibid., 58–59.

12. Michael Hammer and James Champy, *Reengineering the Corporation*, 32.

13. Ibid., 49.

5

THE CONSEQUENCES

◨

Shaping the Inner Spirit

Everything we do has a consequence. Most of us learn that early in life. When you fall, it hurts. When you laugh, it feels good. Consequences like these naturally follow in a cause-and-effect relationship. But as we get older, the consequences are not so clearly defined.

A friend of mine called me one day. "Tom," he said, "I wish you'd explain my son to me. I sat down with him at the beginning of the school year and said, 'Son, don't you want to get straight *A*s, bring the family name some glory, and make your old pop proud?'"

His son answered, "Well sure, Dad, I have feelings like that, but they pass quickly."

My friend explained that this is the same kid who spends six hours a day practicing football in August when it's 110 degrees in the shade and there isn't a speck of shade in sight. What my friend really wanted to know was this—why was his son willing to work so hard for one thing and let another potential success pass him by?

That's easy. It's the power of consequences.

In football, you huddle up with your teammates and the quarterback calls your number to receive. You go out fifteen yards, in front of three thousand of your peers—and when the ball comes to you, you drop it. Now you know what happens next—three thousand of your peers scream, "Get that guy out of the game!"

But football is often forgiving. A few minutes later, the play is called again. And this time, you go out fifteen yards, catch the ball, and run for a touchdown. Those same three thousand peers are now cheering your name. They were cheering your name from the moment you caught, not dropped, that ball.

Is that a consequence a teenage boy is going to work for? He'd die for it. Is that a consequence that getting straight *A*s is going to bring him? Probably not.

The person who receives the consequence is the person who decides how good, bad, or indifferent that consequence is. To my friend, straight *A*s conjured up all kinds of excellent consequences—scholarships, good colleges, and an incredible feeling of pride. But to his son, the idea of a packed stadium wildly chanting his name felt a whole lot better.

Let's compare that scenario to a day at work. Say it's been a really good day. You started the morning by unloading a nonperformer you've been trying to get rid of for a year. You finessed your way around a couple of sticky situations and found the solution to a problem that's been plaguing the company for months.

When you get ready to leave that evening, the entire staff is lined up at the door, cheering your name wildly. Right?

Wrong. In organizational life, it takes forever to reward someone for good work. In fact, most days it isn't rewarded at all. But we never forget a dropped ball or a mistake. Because of that, multitudes of organizations in America today are in a state of paralysis. Why? Because every member of the organization is afraid of making a mistake.

Yet if most of us were to look over our careers and our lives, we would probably say that the old adage is true: we learn the most from our mistakes—especially when those mistakes are handled in a positive, encouraging, nurturing way by someone who wants to help us continually improve.

Myron Rush tells this wonderful story in *Management: A Biblical Approach*:

One morning the divisional manager of a wholesale firm invited me to breakfast. Halfway through the bacon and eggs, he said, "I wanted to talk with you because I'm afraid I'm about to be fired from my job." I was shocked because I had recently conducted a management training program for him and several of his supervisors. I had been impressed with his managerial insights and abilities.

"What's the problem?" I asked.

"Well," he began, "this past year I failed to keep my inventory under control. As a result, my division ended the year several hundred-thousand dollars in the red." He was obviously upset and took a deep breath as he concluded. "I received a call from the president yesterday saying he wants to talk with me. I'm flying back to our corporate office tomorrow to meet with him—I assume to be fired."

I offered the manager what few encouraging words I could and told him I would call him if I heard of any jobs he might want.

Three days later, he called and said, "I thought I should let you know I don't need another job. The president wanted to meet me personally to assure me he still had confidence in my ability to manage the division. He thought I probably needed some encouragement as a result of the bad year I had just experienced." He ended the conversation by saying, "One thing is certain, I don't intend to let my boss down. If he thinks I can do the job, I'll prove he's right."

The next year his division earned the largest profit in the entire corporation. I have had several conversations with him since that incident. More than once he has indicated that knowing his boss trusts him has given him the confidence and motivation needed to develop a highly productive group of employees.[1]

Equally significant, I'll bet that all the money in the world could not buy a higher level of loyalty and commitment than this individual feels for this company. He believes in his company because it believes in him.

In a speech on the fear of failure, Lawrence Appley, former president of the American Management Association, says:

What is so terrible about making a mistake? It is from our mistakes that we learn. Without mistakes there can be no progress. It is hard to realize why the almost paralyzing fear of error curbs the initiative of so many . . . in management. This fear of error is one of the main reasons for costly red tape and controls that are established to insure against errors which, if made, could not cost anywhere near as much as the controls do.[2]

In *Bringing Out the Best in People,* Aubrey C. Daniels describes behavioral consequences as those things and events that follow a behavior and change the probability that the behavior will be repeated in the future. "People do what they do because of what happens to them when they do it."[3]

Four consequences change behavior. *Positive reinforcement* and *negative reinforcement* tend to increase behavior. *Extinction* and *punishment* tend to decrease it.

Consequence:	Result:	Name:
Getting something you want	Increase	Positive Reinforcement
Avoiding something you don't want	Increase	Negative Reinforcement
Not getting something you don't want	Decrease	Extinction
Getting something you don't want	Decrease	Punishment

POSITIVE REINFORCEMENT: MAXIMIZING PERFORMANCE

The consequence that is most effective in increasing a performance or behavior is *positive reinforcement.*

Positive reinforcement is used a great deal today in schools, parenting, and business. It refers to getting something you want (the positive) and strengthening something that is already there (the reinforcement).

If you put iron into a concrete girder that runs across the ceiling, you strengthen it. That is why it is called reinforced concrete. Similarly, if you join a positive consequence to a behavior in such a way that a person associates the consequence with the behavior, then you're reinforcing—or strengthening—it. If that person says, "I like that consequence. It's positive and rewarding. I want more of it," you are practicing positive reinforcement.

Tangible reinforcement might include raises, cash awards, trips, a day off—things that are of monetary value to a person. *Intangible* rewards might be plaques, trophies, thank-you notes, and—most important—expressions of appreciation, praise, and recognition. Intangible rewards don't cost you a dime but can become the most valuable reinforcers you'll ever use.

Performance-Based

Praise and recognition must be based on performance. If you are going around praising everybody but nothing is actually getting much better, are you practicing positive reinforcement? No, because you are not strengthening positive behavior but are simply handing out random undeserved praise.

Knowledgeable

Praise and recognition must be seen as coming from someone who is actually knowledgeable about what the person is contributing. If you don't know a great deal about the work you are praising, take the time to study it. Understand it well enough that your praise shows that you know what's involved in truly doing the job well.

Frequent

Praise and recognition must be given frequently. I once had a client ask, "Don't you think you'll ruin people if you praise them too much?" (And he was the manager of whom it was said, "I've worked for that guy for over seventeen years. I haven't had a compliment yet.") Most managers could increase their use of positive reinforcement fivefold starting tomorrow and they wouldn't be overdoing it, providing it is based on actual performance.

Many men in our culture have been raised to believe that there's something wimpy about sincerely praising people. Women supervisors instinctively seem to be better at using positive reinforcement than their male counterparts. Men would like a system to do it for them.

It's like the man who took his wife to the doctor because she was depressed and run-down. The doctor said, "I want to see you both, together, tomorrow afternoon." They came in, and the doctor startled them both when he leaped out of his chair, bounded around his desk, lifted the woman out of her chair and into his arms, kissed her, and said, "Darling, I think you're the most wonderful person in the world, and I can't imagine living my life without you."

The woman sat down, and the doctor returned to his desk and said, "Now, sir, *that* is all your wife needs three times a week to feel better."

To which the husband replied, "Doc, I'm glad we straightened that out. Now, do you want me to bring her in on Mondays, Wednesdays, and Fridays?"

That's just a story, but it illustrates a fundamental law of behavior. Systems do not reinforce people; only people reinforce people. People will work harder and longer for the sincere praise, admiration, and recognition of a supervisor they respect than for almost any other single thing.

Timely

Praise and recognition must be immediate. Organizational psychologist Paul Brown says:

> Other things being equal, the more immediate the reinforcement, the more powerful it is in terms of strengthening behavior. This is why a smile, a word of thanks, a brief conversation over a cup of coffee are all more powerful than a gold watch at the end of 25 years of "Meritorious Service." Skilled managers are vigilant in looking for achievements to recognize and reinforce. They get a lot of mileage out of the small things they do because they know

the value of immediate reinforcers. . . . Savvy managers use their own words of appreciation and other social reinforcers to bridge the gap between the completion of some task and the delivery of larger, more tangible reinforcers.[4]

Specific to the Person

Praise and recognition should be specific to the person. Strong leaders take time to find out what is reinforcing to each individual. They don't assume they know. In one company, a middle manager called the wife of one of his employees and found out that the employee had always wanted to build a grandfather clock. The employee was extremely touched when the kit was presented at an informal breakfast meeting. That manager knew the value of personalizing reinforcers.

NEGATIVE REINFORCEMENT: MINIMUM PERFORMANCE

The opposite of positive reinforcement is *negative reinforcement*. In negative reinforcement, the person already has something he wants—say, a job—and a negative reinforcer is warning him that he is going to lose it if his performance doesn't improve to an acceptable standard.

The problem with negative reinforcement is easy to see. It produces a just-enough-to-get-by level of performance—not what most of us are looking for in our employees. Yet that is exactly what many companies in this country are seeing. Minimum performance at best. Why? Because of the four consequences available, negative reinforcement is the only one many managers and supervisors use.

Follow Through on Your Warnings

This doesn't mean that negative reinforcement has no place in organizations. Negative reinforcement is a warning, and some people need warnings. But here is a warning about warnings: Never issue a warning unless you absolutely intend to carry it out. If there is no improvement and you don't follow through, you've got the worst of all worlds. You've created a negative culture by dishing out half-baked negative warnings, and your credibility is zero because you never follow through. That's when you end up with a group of employees saying, "Forget it. Just pretend you never heard it. They don't really mean what they say."

But when you mean business, there are certainly times when it is absolutely appropriate to go to a person and use a "do this or else" ultimatum. It's like the time I lost some money on a bad investment. I came home and I said to my wife, "What if I lost *all* of our money? I'm just sort of curious—would you still love me?"

She said, "Tom, let me put it this way. And, honey, I've never meant anything more in my life. I'd always love you, but I'd miss you." That's negative reinforcement.

Reward Improvement

When things improve, support that improvement. You know what I'm talking about here—when things have really slipped, a supervisor goes out and starts chewing people out and having those infamous do-better-or-heads-are-going-to-roll sessions.

In the short term, things may get better. But here's the critical point. If improvement is made, you must support that improvement with positive reinforcement along the way, or you'll be right back where you started. Performance will keep going downhill until you warn the employees again.

That is not what you want. Continuous improvement of all work processes is the name of the game—and to achieve that you must pick up on improvements and praise those immediately when they occur.

If quality keeps rising to a minimum standard and then declines, you can bet there's an overdependence on negative reinforcement and an underutilization of positive reinforcement.

NOTHING IS SOMETHING: EXTINGUISHING PERFORMANCE

Although negative reinforcement is used too frequently in organizations, the most common consequence that people experience on the job is *extinction*.

Extinction happens when a behavior occurs but reinforcement does not follow. Some people say that extinction is the absence of a consequence. A better way of saying it is that "nothing" *is* a consequence.

Think about it. If you have an employee who is really trying to be more conscientious, detail oriented, or responsive to customers, and nobody ever says anything about that improvement—not even a simple "thanks"—that's a consequence. It's not just the absence of a consequence.

All you have to do to influence human behavior is absolutely nothing. The fact is, doing absolutely nothing usually has the biggest impact on human behavior.

It's like the husband who said to his new wife, "I told you I loved you when I married you. If I change my mind, I'll let you know." That marriage is on the downhill already.

Here's another example I hear constantly. "My people know that no news is good news." Do they? I'm afraid not. People always interpret no news as bad news—every time. If they don't hear anything at all from management, they assume that management must not be very impressed with what they're doing.

Perhaps you can relate to this story.

I was in a Dallas hotel one day, and I went down to get a soft drink out of the machine. I put four quarters in and hit the button. What consequence did I want? I wanted a Diet Coke® to jump out down there. You know what happened instead—nothing.

So I did what any well-trained psychologist would do. I kicked the machine. Still, nothing. Then I did something really silly. I reached into my pocket, found four more quarters, and fed them into the machine. I hit the button one more time and got nothing.

Now let me tell you, I was not about to put four more quarters into that machine!

People do not persist very long in putting "coins" into their jobs if they get nothing in return. Yet in too many organizations, the only thing you get from doing quality work—is nothing. In fact, I would say that the two most common consequences for doing good work are nothing at all or more work to do! That's extinction.

PUNISHMENT: A NEGATIVE CONSEQUENCE

The fourth consequence is one that I don't really like to discuss. I don't know many people who do. It is difficult to use, but it has to be there. It's called *punishment*.

Punishment is getting something you don't want. It says you may not go below this level without receiving a negative consequence. In organizational life that usually means a demotion, suspension, or termination.

Of course, these days, when we fire people, it tends to be a happy hunting ground for attorneys, who are well aware of the fact that we haven't kept good data on performance. That is why most organizations should not work first on firing people. They need instead to put a performance-tracking system into place that really shows what people are doing and gives an individual the opportunity to improve behavior and receive positive reinforcement.

But when you've done the best you can with an individual and there is no improvement in sight, then you have to opt for replacement, because a team anybody can play on isn't much of a team at all.

What are some legitimate reasons for terminating an employee?

Dishonesty

Termination should be used in the case of dishonest behavior. This would incude such things as stealing company property or funds, submitting false expense reports, or deliberately lying.

Abuse of Employees, Co-workers

No worker should be allowed to physically or sexually abuse another employee. To tolerate this is to reward it.

Safety Violations

Employees who consistently refuse to follow safety procedures should be terminated. No employee has the right to make the workplace dangerous for others.

Breach of Confidentiality

Giving away corporate secrets or confidential strategies to a competitor is grounds for termination.

Rude Treatment of Customers

Employees who consistently treat customers in a rude, offensive manner should be replaced quickly.

When There Is No Improvement

Continuous improvement is not an option. If an employee's performance is far below the rest of the group and shows no upward trend, replace him. Otherwise, you're not being fair to the others.

When All Else Fails

When you've done all you can, and there is no improvement, you must terminate. Don't beat yourself up thinking that if only you had more time you could change this person. You're probably wrong. Besides, you're not running a clinic, you're running an organization. Take yourself off the hook. You've done your best. Let the employee start over somewhere else. *You* start over with someone who wants to be part of a quality team.

Bringing Behavior to a Stop

But if you're going to punish, you need to be realistic about what you're going to accomplish. The only purpose of punishment is to bring unacceptable behavior to a stop. It is psychologically impossible to punish people into higher levels of performance. On the other hand, punishment is very effective in bringing unacceptable behavior to a stop.

That is why I believe most discussions on capital punishment are off base. Capital punishment doesn't make the rest of the "bad guys" better. It is effective, however, in bringing one person's behavior to a stop. So far as I know, no one who has experienced capital punishment has committed another crime. That's punishment.

MADE IN JAPAN

Let me give you an example of behavioral consequences in Japan. If you worked for a Japanese company, and it got into serious trouble and had to lay off workers, here's what would happen.

Your supervisor would call you in and say, "I'm sorry, but you're on layoff status." On the following work day, you'd come back in and do the same job, except you'd perform at your highest level and with as much creativity as possible. And at the end of the week, you'd get a check. Now this check would be at a reduced level, because the company was experiencing financial difficulties, but you would still get the check. You could still live on your income if you were frugal.

The company would then turn around and bill the Japanese government for your check, because you were on layoff status.

The philosophy of the Japanese government is that if a company gets into trouble, the last thing the government needs to do is pay people to sit at home. The smartest thing it can do is to pay people to help get that company out of trouble.

Then, when the company gets out of trouble and returns to profitability, that money becomes a long-term loan that is repaid into a pool that will help other companies experiencing similar problems.

Whether you agree with the Japanese system or not, it has one great advantage: No work, no pay. That's the power of consequences.

TRUTH AND CONSEQUENCES

We learn right from wrong in the family structure as we receive positive reinforcement, warnings, and discipline. We develop our sense of identity, our goals, and our vision of who we are and what we can become from our parents, our teachers, and various authority figures.

I was raised in a home where the parents took the position

that "if you're in a little trouble at school, you're in a whole lot of trouble at home." I knew it was important to respect my teachers, obey certain rules, study hard, do homework, and get something accomplished every day. I often failed to meet their standards (or my own), but I never doubted that there were standards—and consequences.

This message was conveyed in an atmosphere that let me know that no failure is final and that I was still cared for and valued even when I wasn't an angel (which was most of the time). At the time, I had no appreciation for the importance of any of this to my emotional, spiritual, or moral development—and even rebelled against it—but eventually I came to see the value of what my parents were trying to teach me.

The situation is quite different today. If you say to an American student, "Look, you have to do your homework and master your lessons because if you don't study and learn, you won't be promoted," I can almost guarantee that he will reply, "Oh, no, I don't have to work. Everybody gets promoted."

If you say to the person standing outside your home trying to get inside to steal your stereo, "Don't do that, or you'll go to prison," he's going to reply, "Oh, no, I've got a seventy-five percent chance of not getting caught at all, and if they do catch me, I've got a thirty-five percent chance of not going to prison."

Only 68 percent of American youth graduate from high schools, and corporations are finding that substantial numbers of their employees are functionally illiterate. The average length of employment for teenagers in the fast-food business is seven weeks. By then they have to be replaced for missing too much work.

These symptoms are the result of raising a generation in a world free of consequences. They are the natural outcome in a society that no longer holds people accountable for moral behavior. Yet unless we rediscover our moral souls and recognize the power of consequences, we will never realize the potential of the human spirit.

Every business leader in America needs to get involved in improving the quality of public education and speaking out for an education that includes moral values. H. James Harrington, a principal in the firm of Ernst & Young, says:

To have real impact, the quality professional's focus has to be on improving the quality of our children's lives before and after they enter schools. Sure, we can do a lot to error-proof our process, making it difficult to provide bad products and services, but to excel, we need to be proud of ourselves and the organizations that we work for. We need to develop a future generation that takes pride in what they are doing no matter how menial the activities. Excellence is paying meticulous attention to detail, and we need to excel.[5]

Attention to moral excellence needs to be a feature of our civic society as well. Robert Amsden, a member of the business faculty of the University of Dayton, asks:

Are we using quality concepts and thinking to understand and correct the blight of our cities? How can we reconcile respect for people, a basic tenet of TQM, and abortion? How can we expect our children to learn to be quality citizens when in our public schools we disregard our Judeo-Christian heritage and ignore Aristotle's and Plato's definitions of good education?[6]

The debate today on these issues is often framed in political terms—a leftist-rightist argument—but politics has nothing to do with it. The issue is much more profound. A February 1995 issue of *Newsweek* was devoted to the question raised on its cover: "Shame: How Do We Bring Back a Sense of Right and Wrong?" Some of the quotes in the article reflect a significant shift in perspective from the "social engineering" solutions of the past.

Kathleen Sylvester of the Progressive Policy Institute, a centrist Democratic think tank, comments in the *Newsweek* article: "We need to say that it's shameful to bring a child into the world and not be able to support, love and care for it."[7] Sociologist Amitai Etzioni, author of *The Spirit of Community*, reminds us of a forgotten fact: that "[erring] on the side of self-righteousness" is better than being "immobilized by a fear of being considered prudish."[8]

David Blankenhorn, author of an important new book, *Fatherless America*, agrees: "A stronger sense of shame about illegitimacy and divorce would do more than any tax cut, or any new government program, to improve the life circumstances of children. Compassion doesn't mean accepting whatever other people do. And judgment doesn't mean being hard-hearted."[9]

Richard John Neuhaus thinks we began to lose our sense of right and wrong not in the 1960s, as is often argued, but in the Pollyanna 1950s, when spiritual leaders proclaimed, says Neuhaus, that "you could have a positive side without the negative, which is philosophically and practically impossible." Neuhaus adds:

> We *should* dislike much about ourselves, because there is much about ourselves that is not only profoundly dislikable, but odious. It's not for nothing that the Ten Commandments are put in the negative.[10]

This same issue of *Newsweek* contains an astonishing and refreshing essay by Kenneth L. Woodward entitled "What Ever Happened to Sin?" In it, he says:

> All religions remind us that actions have consequences for which guilt can and must be acknowledged, forgiveness humbly begged, reconciliation sought. Sin is evil, knowingly willed and done. But, like virtue, sin results from habits that take time to develop, and even longer to overcome. Sin, moralists tell us, is a disease of the soul, not a passing headache. And if the Scriptures are to be believed, there is more rejoicing in heaven over one contrite sinner than over 99 righteous who have no need of repentance.[11]

These experts are calling us back to a world in which people can grow into mature moral beings nurtured in an environment of consistent standards and consequences. If we are to succeed in this quest, we will also need something we'll discuss in the next chapter—skill in affirming and reinforcing the right behaviors.

REFERENCES

1. Myron D. Rush, *Management: A Biblical Approach* (Wheaton, Ill.: Scripture Press, Victor Books, 1983), 36–37.
2. Lawrence Appley, quoted in *Management: A Biblical Approach*, 39.
3. Aubrey C. Daniels, *Bringing Out the Best in People: How to Apply the Astonishing Power of Positive Reinforcement* (New York: McGraw-Hill, 1993), 25.

4. Paul Brown, *Managing Behavior on the Job: Performance Improvement* (New York: Wiley, 1982), 109.

5. H. James Harrington, quoted in Scott Madison Patow, "New Gurus: The Next Leaders of the Quality Revolution," *Quality Digest*, March 1995, 31.

6. Robert Amsden, quoted in "New Gurus: The Next Leaders of the Quality Revolution," 35.

7. Kathleen Sylvester, quoted in Jonathan Alter and Pat Wingert, "The Return of Shame," *Newsweek*, 6 February 1995, 24.

8. Amitai Etzioni, *The Spirit of Community: Rights, Responsibilities, and the Communitarian Agenda* (New York: Random House, Crown Publishing, 1993), quoted in Alter and Wingert, "The Return of Shame," 25.

9. David Blankenhorn, quoted in Alter and Wingert, "The Return of Shame," 25.

10. Richard John Neuhaus, quoted in Alter and Wingert, "The Return of Shame," 22.

11. Kenneth L. Woodward, "What Ever Happened to Sin?" *Newsweek*, 6 February 1995, 23.

6

THE REWARDS

◪

Satisfying the Inner Spirit

Any behavior that is rewarded is likely to be repeated. That is basic common sense. Why, then, do people find it so hard to put that truism into practice? Why is it so difficult for managers and parents and teachers to appropriately reward the kind of behavior they want to see more of?

Go to the "parenting" section of any library or bookstore and you'll find volumes on the subject of rewarding good behavior. The shelves are stacked with suggestions for using sticker charts, trips to the zoo, even cold, hard cash as reinforcement. But, again, many parents will tell you that these methods just don't work. The same is true for managers. I can't tell you the number of times I've heard someone say, "I've tried rewarding employees—you know, giving positive reinforcement—and it just doesn't work."

I think I know why. They simply don't know how. They don't know how to put the power of positive reinforcement to work. Positive reinforcement does work. In fact, it will astonish you as to how well it works. But knowing how to reinforce and reward effectively is a learned skill.

Let me tell a true story that will help illustrate this point. A few years ago I started working in a production facility and said,

"Who is the worst worker in the place? Who would you like to fire this week?"

The answer was immediate. "That's easy. It's Smitty."

"What's wrong with Smitty?"

"Well, we've been studying Smitty for the last two weeks, and what we've discovered is that about eighteen percent of everything Smitty makes is junk. As a matter of fact, he's keeping an entire quality control department busy, just straightening out his lousy work."

"How long has Smitty been with you?"

"He's never been *with* us, he's been *against* us from the start. But we've been paying him for eighteen months." I'll never forget that answer.

"OK, I'll work with Smitty. But three things have to change. First, if Smitty messes it up, Smitty straightens it out. He fixes his own mistakes. Second, I want you to put a clipboard at Smitty's workstation and have him count the number of things that come back to him every day."

That may sound pretty basic, but I'm continually amazed at how rare these two practices are. If a person is not required to fix the things he messes up and if he doesn't have a clue as to how often he's messing up in the first place, how can anyone expect him to improve the quality of his work?

The third request was directed specifically to Smitty's supervisor. "Jerry, I want you to go by Smitty's workstation every day for a month. I want you to look at his clipboard, and if there is the slightest improvement, even a fraction, I want you to say, 'Hey, Smitty, you're improving. You're doing better. Thank you.' And, if his quality has gone down that day, I still want you to be positive. I want you to say, 'Smitty, I see you're going to have a better day tomorrow,' or something along those lines. I don't care what you say, as long as it's totally positive, every day for a month."

He was an old-school manager, and I'll never forget his tough and salty response. But he agreed to do it.

The next step was mine. I went to Smitty and had a frank conversation with him. "Smitty, do you know that the quality of your work is totally unacceptable?"

You know what he said to me? He said the same thing that I

hear 99 percent of the time. "No, I didn't know that. Nobody has ever discussed it with me." Then he said to me with real concern, "I don't want to lose my job."

That very day, Smitty started doing his work over, straightening out his own messes. He began learning from his mistakes. And he began to improve, first a little, then a lot.

And Jerry ran right over and started giving him the reward he deserved—praise and recognition. Right? Wrong. Now, as you can imagine, I was exasperated with Jerry. "It's ridiculous for your company to pay me this kind of money when you won't go do the one thing that won't cost a dime and is essential to improvement."

"OK. I'll do it." And he marched out of the room and was back in a flash. He hadn't even had time to get to Smitty's workstation, so I knew something was up.

That's when Jerry came clean. "Tom, let me ask you a question. In a case like this, what would I say?"

You see, he didn't have the skill. He'd been managing people for more than twenty-five years, and he didn't know how to praise and recognize an employee.

Right then and there, I sat down with Jerry and wrote out some compliments on three-by-five cards, and we practiced. Finally, Jerry was ready. He walked out and said, "Smitty, let me see your clipboard. Hey, you're doing better. That's great. I just want to say 'thank you and keep up the good work.'"

When Jerry was through, he was shaking like a leaf. But in that moment, I gained tremendous respect for him—because he was doing one of the hardest things there is to do in this world. He was trying to change. Not somebody else, but himself.

There are two terrific endings to this story. The first is that within eleven days, Smitty became the best employee in the plant. He still is today. But I think the second ending is even more inspiring. Jerry changed. And when his employees saw that he could change, they knew that they could too. Within eighteen months, daily manufacturing was up 35 percent. The number of units produced without errors improved 60 percent, despite higher standards. The bottom line improved by $8 million.

You see, Jerry mastered the skill. He learned how to reinforce effectively. He also learned another law of quality performance: *The only person's behavior I can change is my own.*

Dwight D. Eisenhower often said that leadership is the art of getting someone else to do something you want done because he wants to do it. He understood that beyond the science there is an art to leading and managing people—people with hearts and souls and dreams and incredible spirits just waiting to be tapped.

So how do we tap them? How do we inspire them to be their very best? That is the art of rewarding.

TANGIBLE VERSUS INTANGIBLE (SOCIAL) REWARDS

In the previous chapter on consequences and the inner spirit, we talked about tangible reinforcers versus intangible, or social, reinforcers. Aubrey Daniels discusses this difference:

> Social reinforcement is reinforcement that involves doing or saying something to another. [It] includes symbolic reinforcement and anything that has trophy value. In this context, trophy value means that the trophy or symbolic reinforcer would have value only to the person receiving it. It's the most available form of created reinforcement. You don't have to budget for it; you don't need permission to give it. And when given correctly, people never tire of it.
>
> Tangible reinforcement is a positive reinforcer that has salvage value, that is, something that would have value to someone else.[1]

Tangible reinforcement should be used to back up intangible reinforcers. If you keep telling someone that he is doing a good job and that you appreciate his efforts, ultimately he is going to expect some tangible sign of appreciation to back up your intangible, social reinforcer. Tangibles increase the value of social reinforcers.

Every time someone earns a tangible reinforcement, the manager can personally reinforce the employee by praising his performance. In that way the tangible reward—cash, for example—is made a symbol of recognition for achievement and gains maximum value.

We have completely divorced salary increases from any feeling of recognition for individual or team achievement. If you asked one hundred average workers why their companies gave them an increase last year, I'll bet that at least ninety would reply, "To keep me up with the cost of living."

We have not only divorced raises from individual and team achievement, we have divorced them from company success. Too many workers believe the company can have a bad year and still provide raises to everyone. I have even seen employees demanding higher wages from companies about to become insolvent.

That is why our firm offers an exciting training program called *Business Literacy.* Using a board game approach (like Monopoly®), employees learn how cash actually flows through an organization. It's a program in great demand.

SELECTING EFFECTIVE REINFORCERS

I've said it before, but it is worth repeating: The receiver of a consequence is the one who determines whether that consequence is reinforcing. And everybody is different. Different employees will find different things reinforcing. The right word spoken at the right time may be more effective with a particular employee than a raise in salary would be. And poorly selected reinforcers (rewards given across the board to all employees, for example) can backfire and turn into extinction or punishment, regardless of the manager's good intentions.

Bob Nelson, in *One Thousand One Ways to Reward Employees,*[2] gives numerous ideas for reinforcers. I have included ideas elsewhere in this book. In my company's *PRIDE Quality Management Training* program we offer the following four ways to find rewards that will effectively reinforce high performance:

1. Ask people what they like.
2. Observe what people do.
3. Observe what people talk about.
4. Test a reinforcer by trial and error, and see if it works.

In my experience, number one may not always be effective. Employees may not be willing to reveal what they find reinforcing, especially in a questionnaire or interview situation. They may be skeptical as to why you want to know this personal information. Also, they may not actually know what they find reinforcing. After all, it's not the sort of thing a person is asked every day. And finally, they may simply tell you what they think you want to hear.

The best way to find excellent reinforcers is by paying attention to people. Observe what they do when they have a choice. Listen to what they talk about. Do they talk about their families, their boats, or their gardens? Find out how they spend their weekends and vacations.

I once worked with a man who was in a mind-numbing, boring job. He'd lost interest in it, and it showed. Well, I found out that this same man spent every Sunday morning teaching the largest men's Bible class in Atlanta. What do you think he valued most? It was that class.

So I told his supervisor, "Every day he improves, go by and ask him about his class. Ask him what the lesson was last Sunday or what's coming up this week."

And that is exactly what he did. Every time the supervisor mentioned that class, this worker lit up like a Christmas tree. And his work just kept getting better and better. To him, that was a powerful reinforcer. It was rewarding. It said to him, "I'm special. I'm a person here. They know I have brains."

For some people, a piece of new equipment would be absolutely wonderful. And if it were given to them by a supervisor who said, "I'm giving you this because you've shown great improvement," that could be a significant reward.

A company in Kansas City, Missouri, employs eight hundred writers and artists in one building. (How would you like to supervise eight hundred artists? An officer of the company told me it was like herding cats.) For that particular group, the things valued most were individuality, freedom of expression, and creativity. It would be a whole lot easier to simply hand those artists a bonus check or a toaster, but that would be a lot less effective.

Once you have identified the proper reinforcers, make sure you are being practical. Face it, most of us would love to reward our employees with all sorts of terrific things, but we do have to make a profit. So before you start handing out weekly trips to Europe, run your reinforcers past this five-point checklist:

1. *Is it readily available?* This is where intangible reinforcers really shine. A sincere thank-you, a note of appreciation, or a few moments of individual attention are always within reach.

2. *Can it be used frequently?* Employees will never complain about receiving too much praise and recognition. Chances are, they also won't complain about enjoying too many catered lunches, special coffee break snacks, or other little celebrations. They probably won't complain about too many days off, either, but you might. So think about this one.

3. *Is it cost effective?* The reward needs to match the accomplishment. That doesn't mean you should try to equate the dollar value of the reward with the dollar value of the improvement or accomplishment. After all, it's pretty hard to put a dollar figure on the return on investment you'll receive from a high-performing, motivated employee. But common sense says that you probably won't want to reward a week of perfect attendance the same way you might reward the completion of a grueling, six-month project.

4. *Is it controlled by the manager?* Don't promise anything that is out of your jurisdiction. There is nothing worse than coming up empty-handed and full of excuses.

5. *Is it a proper mix of tangible and intangible reinforcers?* No material reward works unless you couple it with praise and recognition. If you remember nothing else, remember that.

All right, now you're ready. You've listened and paid close attention (and if you really have, you're probably seeing some improvement already), and you've found the perfect mix of tangible and intangible reinforcers for every employee on the payroll. Now it's time to put the power of positive reinforcement to work.

In my experience, six things make positive reinforcement really powerful:

1. *It is personal.* It comes from *you*. It's *I* want to thank you. *I* appreciate you. None of this *we*, or *the company*, or *the management*. That also means that in most cases, the reinforcer needs to come from a direct supervisor or manager, or perhaps a team leader or a team member—just so long as it's someone who is personally knowledgeable about what that person is contributing.

2. *It is given immediately or as soon as possible.* The more closely a reward follows a desired behavior, the more reinforcement it provides. The employee receiving the reward is more likely to know which behavior you're reinforcing and will more strongly associate the reward with the behavior.

Here, again, the maxim applies: The six most deadly words in motivation are *At the end of the year.*

How many of your rewards for high performance come annually, at the end of the year? A motivational system that doesn't kick into place until the end of the year isn't going to have much to do with what people do today.

Let me tell you about an attendance project I helped a manufacturing plant introduce. This plant had three shifts and tremendous attendance problems. They had a lot of trouble with the flu on Mondays and Fridays.

The project we designed was pretty simple. If an employee had perfect attendance for the week, and perfect punctuality, then, on the following Monday, that employee's name would go on the perfect attendance honor roll, making him or her eligible for a prize valued at about $50. Notice the time frame—just one week—and that the prize was immediately awarded the following Monday. If you were ill or absent, on vacation or on personal leave, that was fine, but you just didn't participate that week.

Each shift had its own list and its own winner each week. The employee could choose one of three prizes (each valued at $50): flowers delivered to his home, tickets to a pro football or baseball game, or dinner for two in an area restaurant.

It cost the company a mere $150 dollars a week to run this program. But in the first year alone, the plant estimated a savings of $700,000 from improved attendance and a reduction in sick leave. In the second year, the estimate was closer to $1.3 million. You see, the closer you link the reward to the behavior, the greater the influence.

Do programs like this plateau? Yes, they do. But that doesn't mean it's time to stop the basic program or change the basic philosophy. It is probably just time to change the rewards.

3. *It is specific.* If you want a person to repeat a specific

behavior or performance, you have to reinforce specific behaviors or performance. The reward can't be "For being a great employee and doing a swell job this month." It needs to be "For your careful attention to detail and the exceptional way you're working with the staff, which has resulted in a three percent reduction in errors over the last thirty days." Leave no room for misinterpretation.

4. *It is sincere.* Failing to pair tangible reinforcement with intangible reinforcement makes it seem as if you don't really mean it. It is less sincere—and if the appreciation is not sincere, it's back to nothing: extinction. So you'd better mean it.

And it had better be true. You can never, ever give somebody a reward in the hope that he will improve in the future. That is called bribery. Reinforcers should be given after the improvement occurs.

Parents are sometimes the worst offenders in this. In *Dr. Mom's Parenting Guide: Common Sense Guidance for the Life of Your Child*, Dr. Marianne Neifert, pediatrician and mother of five, says:

A reward is an incentive given for desirable behavior. It's something [to] work toward and feel proud of. A bribe is an advance payoff given either to produce desired behavior, or to stop or prevent misbehavior. The crucial difference is that a bribe is given before the desired behavior, as when you say, "I'll let you sit next to your friend if you agree not to talk in class." Chances are, the two friends will talk plenty. Bribes given in advance are always less effective than either positive or negative reinforcement that is closely linked to behavior.[3]

5. *It is consistent.* This one is really tough. It means that on the day you don't feel good, when you're tired and overwhelmed with a hundred things to do, there will be someone on your staff who needs positive reinforcement, and you're going to make sure they get it. Why? Because yesterday, when you were feeling terrific, you reinforced that employee's co-worker for the very same accomplishment, and you have to be consistent.

John Rosemond emphasizes this point in *John Rosemond's Six-Point Plan for Raising Happy, Healthy Children*.

Consistency makes it possible . . . to predict the consequences of
. . . behavior. The ability to anticipate consequences and adjust
behavior accordingly is essential to the development of self-discipline, which is the ultimate goal of . . . discipline. Without consistency, therefore, discipline isn't discipline. It's confusion.[4]

6. *It is never mixed with criticism.* Violations of this rule are
often referred to as the "sandwich method," because a negative
is usually sandwiched between two positives. It might sound like
this: "Nice job on the presentation this morning. I was disap-
pointed that you didn't use any of the comments I suggested. But
the client seemed pleased." Or even worse: "You're one of the
best employees we've got—when you're here."

This doesn't mean that you can never give criticism. In fact,
employees that are often praised and recognized for their
accomplishments and improvement will usually seek your feedback, because they know it may ultimately lead to more praise
and recognition. Just don't do it in the same breath, or you'll be
wasting it.

THE MILLION-DOLLAR QUESTION

I can't leave the subject of rewards without talking about the
most commonly discussed reward of them all: money.

In chapter 2, I said that it is a myth that money is the primary motivator and the best possible reward. But money can't be
ignored. People work because they need money (which is, ironi-
cally, why it's usually *not* the best reward).

People should be fairly compensated for the work they do,
and this compensation should directly reflect the level and excellence of their work. American companies typically fail to give
monetary rewards on this basis. In *Why TQM Fails and What to
Do About It*, the authors speak to the inadequacies in the compensation system traditionally used in the United States.

Pay systems in most American companies have changed very little since the 1950s. Typically, each position has a compensation
range based on an evaluation of the job and pay scales for similar
positions in similar organizations. The salary an individual
receives falls within the range established for his or her job
grade, with such considerations as length of time with the com-

pany, salary agreed on when the position was accepted, and ability to meet annual goals and objectives factored in.

The salary range for most job grades is narrow. Raises, usually dispensed once a year, typically range from three to seven percent, depending on economic factors and on the organization's financial performance. (Exceptional performers receive the 6 to 7 percent raises, while mediocre performers receive 3 to 4 percent raises.)

The major disadvantage of traditional compensation systems like the one described above is that outstanding performers earn the same, or just slightly more, than average performers. This type of compensation does little or nothing to motivate employees to perform at peak levels. And [it] has very little or nothing to do with quality and customer satisfaction.[5]

Fortunately, there are companies that are successfully using nontraditional compensation systems that integrate quality and customer satisfaction. Federal Express is an excellent example.

Every employee at the company, including officers and the CEO, is put on an incentive-based pay system that uses "people and service" as the primary guidelines for quarterly bonuses. Every quarter, each employee is given a rating by other employees (subordinates or peers) on his performance as a supervisor, manager, or team player. That is how the "people" rating is achieved.

The "service" rating is based on customer satisfaction. Employees who do not deal directly with external customers receive the rating based on internal customer satisfaction.

If an employee does not meet the standard for people or service, he does not receive a quarterly bonus. If he meets the standard, the bonus amount is determined by a system that translates his performance to financial measures and the profit his performance brings to the company.

The icing on Federal Express's incentive-based pay system is the quarterly feedback each employee receives, keeping the focus on satisfied employees, satisfied customers, and a profitable company.

Charles Schwab & Company similarly understands that customer service is what it sells. That is why it pays its people for service, not transactions. Bonuses for managers and for customer contact personnel are based primarily on customer satisfaction surveys.

Another compensation system gaining popularity in this country is pay-at-risk. This plan is similar to the way employees are compensated at most companies in Japan. With pay-at-risk, an employee's compensation is achieved partly from a base salary and partly from a bonus. However, since the bonus is received only if certain performance standards are met, that portion of the pay is at risk. In this scenario, the bonus is not a trivial amount but, rather, a significant portion of the compensation.

Here are some ideas for tangible and intangible reinforcers.

1. Letter of recommendation
2. Permission to work on special projects
3. Verbal praise
4. Letting the person report his results to upper management
5. Allowing the person to make decisions affecting his work
6. Positive comments on performance improvements
7. Memo to supervisors on the performance of subordinates with a copy sent to the subordinate
8. Flex-time
9. Passing along compliments from others
10. Choice of tasks
11. Increased responsibility
12. Removing a constant supervision requirement
13. An early start on vacations
14. Plaques, trophies, diplomas
15. Represent department at meetings
16. Spruce up work area
17. Time off
18. Secretarial service
19. Transfers
20. Quick follow-up on requests, problems, etc.
21. Name on the bulletin board for meeting a goal

22. Asking the person for advice or opinions
23. Free lunch, dinner for two
24. Putting positive information into the employee's personnel folder
25. Raises
26. Exception to a company policy or procedure
27. Training for better jobs
28. Additional help
29. Talking to the employee about personal interests
30. Cup of coffee, donuts, free use of vending machines
31. Parking space
32. Promotions
33. Asking the employee to assist you in some of your duties
34. A thank-you, a nod, a smile, a handshake, a pat on the back
35. Car fare to work
36. A personal phone call or note from you
37. An article with special logo or insignia on it, e.g., coffee mug, pen, tie clip, or pin
38. Work scheduling that is especially tailored to the employee
39. Bonuses
40. Talking to the person about some anticipated positive reinforcer; e.g., "I'll bet you're looking forward to going to the game."
41. First choice at extra training and new equipment or tools
42. Job rotation
43. Listening
44. Fringe benefits
45. Car pool using company vans
46. Gift certificate
47. Clothing, e.g., T-shirts, hats, jackets with special logos

THE SPIRITUAL SIDE OF REWARDS

Some people argue that tangible rewards are like carrots offered to a horse and are therefore demeaning to good workers. Motivation, they say, comes from inside. Others argue that rewards *do* work, and they have reams of data to prove it.

This is a phony debate. What both sides fail to understand is that a meaningful reward combined with meaningful recognition can actually change people *on the inside.* A new set of work values can be born inside a person when he or she enters a positive work culture that insists on the best and rewards it. Motivation comes from within, but it can be powerfully shaped by the external work culture.

In the final analysis, we are talking about something more profound than money or perks. We are talking about something "spiritual": tapping something profound and wonderful inside people. A story from *Chicken Soup for the Soul* makes this point.

> A teacher in New York decided to honor each of her seniors in high school by telling them the difference they each made. Using a process developed by Helice Bridges of Del Mar, California, she called each student to the front of the class, one at a time. First she told [the class] how the student made a difference to her and the class. Then she presented [him] with a blue ribbon imprinted with gold letters which read, "Who I Am Makes a Difference."
>
> Afterwards the teacher . . . gave each of the students three more ribbons and instructed them to go out and spread this acknowledgment ceremony. Then they were to follow up on the results, see who honored whom, and report back to the class in about a week.

One of the boys gave his ribbons to a junior executive in a nearby company who had helped him in his career planning and asked him to pass along the honor. The junior executive gave the ribbons in turn to his boss.

> That night the boss came home to his 14-year-old son [and] said, "The most incredible thing happened to me today. I was in my office and one of the junior executives came in and told me he admired me and gave me a blue ribbon for being a creative genius. Imagine. He thinks I'm a creative genius. Then he put this blue ribbon that says 'Who I Am Makes a Difference' on my jack-

et above my heart. He gave me an extra ribbon and asked me to find somebody else to honor. As I was driving home tonight, I started thinking about whom I would honor with this ribbon, and I thought about you. I want to honor you.

"My days are really hectic, and when I come home I don't pay a lot of attention to you. Sometimes I scream at you for not getting good enough grades in school and for your bedroom being a mess, but somehow tonight, I just wanted to sit here and, well, just let you know that you do make a difference to me. Besides your mother, you are the most important person in my life. You're a great kid and I love you!"

The startled boy started to sob and sob, and he couldn't stop crying. His whole body shook. He looked up at his father and said through his tears, "I was planning on committing suicide tomorrow, Dad, because I didn't think you loved me. Now I don't need to."[6]

So much for whether an external reward can produce internal change!

THE EIGHT LAWS OF QUALITY PERFORMANCE

1. Any behavior that is rewarded is more likely to be repeated.
2. The only person's behavior I can change is my own.
3. Behavior is determined by consequences.
4. People behave on a daily basis because of what happens to them on a daily basis.
5. Doing something or doing nothing can both change behavior.
6. Giving people something for nothing makes them good for nothing.
7. People cannot be punished into higher levels of performance.
8. Systems don't reinforce people—people reinforce people.

REFERENCES

1. Aubrey C. Daniels, *Bringing Out the Best in People: How to Apply the Astonishing Power of Positive Reinforcement* (New York: McGraw-Hill, 1994), 54.

2. Bob Nelson, *One Thousand One Ways to Reward Employees* (New York: Workman, 1994).

3. Marianne Egeland Neifert, *Dr. Mom's Parenting Guide: Common Sense Guidance for the Life of Your Child* (New York: NAL-Dutton, Signet Books, 1991), 145.

4. John K. Rosemond, *John Rosemond's Six-Point Plan for Raising Happy, Healthy Children* (Kansas City, Mo.: Andrews & McMeel-Universal, 1989), 52.

5. Mark Graham Brown, Darcy E. Hitchcock, and Marsha L. Willard, *Why TQM Fails and What to Do About It* (Burr Ridge, Ill.: Irwin Professional, 1994), 131–34.

6. Jack Canfield and Mark Victor Hansen, *Chicken Soup for the Soul: One-Hundred One Stories to Open the Heart and Rekindle the Spirit* (Deerfield Beach, Fla.: Health Communications, 1993), 19–21.

7

THE PROBLEMS
◪
Diagnosing Diseases of the Inner Spirit

Here is a common experience I've had in the consulting business. I'm sitting in my office, and the phone rings. A manager from a distant city calls with a request. The following conversation ensues:

"Would you come out and talk to our staff?"

"What would you like for me to talk to them about?"

"About an hour and a half."

"No, I mean, what topics shall I cover?"

"I'm not sure. How about attitude? That's important, isn't it? Work in something on customer service and sales and employee appearance. And above all, motivate them. They're just not motivated. So, motivate them. OK?"

"That's a tall order for an hour and a half."

"Well, we'd like to give you more time, but their accident rate is terrible, so we've got to really chew them out about safe driving. Then we'll put you on for the motivation part."

Something tells me this isn't going to work. But believe it or not, this is not a caricature. It reflects what I sometimes call the "Ready-Fire-Aim" school of management. It's very easy for an organization to apply an expensive solution before it has even defined the problem.

During the Second World War, Allied airplanes were being shot down in great numbers over Germany. The surviving airplanes limped back to England streaming smoke and fuel and barely making it to safety. The military began studying these planes to see where they were taking the most severe shrapnel hits and incurring the greatest damage.

They decided to put extra armor plating on those precise spots before sending the plane back into harm's way. They even began placing extra armor plating on the new airplanes as they rolled off the assembly line.

One day a pilot happened to be in the manufacturing plant, observed this process, and asked why it was being done. When it was explained, he told them that it was precisely the wrong strategy. Can you guess why?

When you think about it, it's perfectly obvious. The strategy was based on the planes that got back. But, in reality, no extra armor plating was needed on the spots that had been hit on those planes. It was the other parts of the surface that needed the extra protection, for if you got hit there, you didn't come back.

What is important to see here is that if we make a wrong assumption in our problem-analysis phase, we will waste our efforts in the problem-solving phase. For example, it seems logical that if a product is inspected repeatedly, it will be perfect. Right? Wrong! The truth is that the more a product is inspected, the more the original producer or assembler assumes, "If I make a mistake, someone else will catch it." The quality of workmanship can actually decline.

Furthermore, the folks who work in inspection or quality control may actually hope that quality won't improve too much, or their very function will be threatened. One group is being rewarded for production, the other for fixing problems. The more products produced by the first group, the better they look. The more problems fixed by the second group, the better they look. All the consequences are on the side of mediocrity; none are on the side of excellence. The groups pay lip service to quality; neither group really wants it.

Years ago, two corporations held major management retreats during the summer months. They even met at the same hotel, one in June, the other in July. The corporations were in identical sectors, what we used to call the dime-store business. Both had the same essential problem. It was costing them sixty cents in overhead expense to sell each fifty cents' worth of merchandise. One does not have to be a financial wizard to predict the future for such a business.

The president of the first organization assigned his leadership group to teams. They were to analyze the problem from every conceivable angle and come back with honest, creative, hard-hitting recommendations to solve the problem, irrespective of turf or tradition.

That's exactly what they did. They recommended closing two hundred small stores and opening over a hundred new stores in the next five years. The new stores would be thirty to fifty times larger. That would require different store designs, products, buyers, and advertising. In short, the teams recommended becoming a different company in five years. The president was stunned, but he could see the wisdom of the recommendations. The company set out to make the changes.

The second company faced the same problem, went through the same process, and came up with a completely different solution. It embarked on a large-scale campaign to modernize its existing stores. It redecorated them, put in carpeting, installed background music, refurbished counters, and improved the lighting. When the job was finished, the company had a beautiful chain of stores. Customers came and were impressed by the surroundings. Everything was great! But there was just one small problem. Now it was costing the company seventy cents in overhead expense to sell each fifty cents' worth of merchandise. The company had exacerbated the very problem it set out to solve.

The first company was known in those days as the S. S. Kresge Company. Through its national system of Kmarts®, it became one of the top retail businesses in the U.S. The second company was known as the W. T. Grant Company, which slid into bankruptcy within three years. That's the difference a good strategy makes. It's not enough to work hard; you also have to work smart.

The irony of the story, of course, is that Kmart proceeded to lose touch with subsequent changes in retailing and allowed Sam Walton to capture much of its traditional market. Today, Kmart is fighting hard to regain its losses. Yesterday's strategy produces yesterday's results.

In our seminars we like to distinguish these three words:

Efficiency

Effectiveness

Excellence

Efficiency is the school of management that places primary emphasis on *doing things right.* It stresses forms, procedures, audits, and inspections. Everything must be done correctly.

Effectiveness is the school of management that places primary emphasis on *doing right things.* Of course, if we're not doing the right things, how we do them becomes a moot point.

Excellence is what all successful organizations are shooting for today. Excellence is *doing the right things right.* In other words, you must focus on those few right things you must do to succeed and do those at the level of excellence.

To stay at a level of excellence, organizations must be alert for competitive threats, and they must become extremely proficient at problem solving and analysis. This last area is a crucial point. Over the years, I have become convinced that it is where American managers need to do better. Our American love of action tends to send us off in all directions without going through the discipline of analysis, data gathering, and good decision making, and so we put these off. Or we may associate problem solving with having done something wrong or see problem solving in terms of placing blame and so fail to act. Now we must face the consequences.

Richard Johnson lists ten essentials in effective problem solving in his book *TQM: Mechanics of Quality Processes.*

1. Recognize the problem.
2. Decide who will solve the problem.
3. Define the problem.

4. Take interim action.
5. Determine the root cause.
6. Develop a solution.
7. Prepare an implementation plan.
8. Verify effectiveness.
9. Prevent recurrence.
10. Provide for recognition of participants.[1]

Not every step will be used in every case. Employees working with a problem-solving methodology must adapt the process to fit their organization and the specific problem they are solving.

Our firm is nationally known for a Quality Improvement Process we call PRIDE. PRIDE stands for

Positive

Reinforcement

for

Improvement

based on

Data

focused on

Employees

There's a lot in this acronym. Let's take it in reverse order. It says that the most important people in any organization are the employees. These are the indispensable people, the ones who get the work done. They also have the best ideas for how it can be done better.

Next, PRIDE is a data-driven system. It places great emphasis on meaningful measurement. We must be able to see the trend. Are we getting better? Are we getting worse? Are we going nowhere? It is always one of the three, whether we know it or not. We'll know which it is if we have the right data system.

Improvement is the most beautiful word in the world for those of us in the quality field. The focus is on improvement, not absolute perfection. People don't get perfect; people *do* get better. Helping people get better is what management is all about.

Finally, when people do improve, the one thing they have a right to expect is positive reinforcement. That can be intangible (praise) or tangible (money), but whatever form it takes, it must be there. It is the energy of the quality movement. Show me how and when an organization celebrates success, and I'll show you the soul of that organization. *Positive Reinforcement for Improvement based on Data and focused on Employees*. That's PRIDE. There's nothing we need more in organizational life.

PRIDE teaches a six-step method for problem solving:

1. Determine the area you want to improve.
2. Analyze the cause or source of the problem.
3. Select the best solution and pilot-test this approach.
4. Set a goal for improvement.
5. Determine how you are going to track progress.
6. Determine how you are going to celebrate and reward improvement.

Let's explore these steps in greater depth.

Your first task is to isolate the problem. We call this *pinpointing*. This is not necessarily an easy task. One way to guide a team in focusing on an area for improvement is to have the team use brainstorming techniques to identify as many ideas as possible, recording all ideas and are accepting them initially without judgment or questions, except for clarification.

At the end of the brainstorming activity, there will be some overlap and duplication of ideas. These items should be grouped into broader categories. Then the team should narrow down its choices and select the ones it will work on first.

Sometimes just restating a problem in a different way helps to clarify what is going on. An initial statement might be "People don't come to work on time." A positive restatement of the problem might be, "How do we encourage employees to be on time?" Or we might state a problem as "Too many shipments don't arrive on time." A restatement might be, "How can we increase the percentage of on-time shipments?" This may seem like a trivial step, but it isn't. It avoids finger-pointing and blaming. It turns a negative discussion into a positive one and moves us from the problem to the solution.

Another way to clarify a problem is to restate it based on its cause, then restate the cause as a question. For example, the problem is that Jenny does not complete her work on time. The possible causes of the problem: Her skills are not up to par, she has too many interruptions, she does not know how to set priorities, or she is overloaded with work. To clarify the problem, restate its cause as a question. How do we get Jenny's skills up to par so she can complete work on time? How do we minimize interruptions so that Jenny can get her work completed on time?

Another tool in working with pinpoints is to list the pinpoints you are considering and then list all the possible causes and possible solutions. That will help the team avoid jumping to premature conclusions when looking for the cause and the solution. Then restate your pinpoint as an improvement goal:

To increase on-time shipments by 10 percent before December 31.

Refinement of the goals may come as you develop a clearer understanding of the problem through further analysis and choosing an intervention.

Aubrey Daniels, in *Performance Management*, states that pinpointing is the process of being specific about what people do. The specifics may be either the behaviors of the performer or the results produced by the behaviors. If one is going to be effective in changing or improving performance, one must be able to describe the performance in terms that are specific, observable, and measurable.[2]

It is too vague to say to someone, "You need to improve the

way you deal with customers." But if you say, "When you greet customers it is necessary to smile, look the customer in the eye, and say, 'How may I help you?' within fifteen seconds," that paints a very different picture. It is specific.

In our organization, in order to pinpoint the problem or area for improvement, we ask what we call the "IT" question:

What is *it* that if we upgrade the quality of *it,* do more of *it,* improve the timeliness of *it,* reduce the cost of *it,* will pay off in significant ways for the organization?

If you've studied industrial engineering, you know that this simple question forces us to think about the four fundamental measures of work.

- Quality
- Quantity
- Timeliness
- Cost

Let's talk about quality versus quantity. (Always begin by looking at quality.) I was once asked to design an incentive system to motivate a sales force to make more calls. First, I spent a week making calls with the sales representatives to learn more about their business. The following week I said to the management group, "You don't really want your sales representatives to make more calls. You are fortunate that the working day isn't any longer or by now they might have alienated the entire industry!"

The problem the sales representatives had was quality, not quantity. The selling skills of the representatives needed to be improved before they made any more calls. The pinpoint area was to focus on improving the way they conducted themselves on calls. Once this problem was solved, we worked with them on making more good calls. Their sales increased.

Manufacturing plants often face the same dilemma. Pressure is applied to increase quantity, but the real issue is quality. It is quality problems that are slowing the process down. Rejects and rework are keeping the company from getting the product shipped on time. Speeding up a defective process doesn't improve anything, even quantity. It just produces a bigger mess.

Quantity *can* be an issue. Sometimes people just need to speed up. They need to expect more of themselves. The culture of the company may not be performance-intensive. Usually if quality is fine and quantity is not, there's an incentive problem. People simply do not believe that improving production will get them anything but more tired. A housekeeper in a hotel may not believe that cleaning a room quickly and thoroughly will get her anything other than another room to clean. In that case, why do it?

That is why many employees pick a number somewhere between the least and the most and settle for it. It makes perfect sense to them in terms of the culture they believe they are working in. The problem is that the difference between average productivity and maximum productivity is the difference between being good and being great.

Timeliness is an important measure. It might be the turnaround time on a complex special order or something as simple as returning a phone call promptly. Make no mistake about it— the customer often interprets quality in terms of time.

Cost is the fourth broad area for pinpoints. If costs can be significantly reduced without affecting quality, it must be done. Until recently, the Department of Defense spent $3.5 billion annually on travel and $1.5 billion on the approval process. Clearly, the cost of the approval process was out of proportion to the cost of the function itself. For a business, money saved in cost reduction can fall directly to the bottom line.

The name of the game is not to change an organization. Anyone can do that. The task is to change an organization for the better. The name of the game isn't "to have a TQM program." Every organization has one (or claims it does). The objective is to have a TQM program that produces measurable improvement in one or more of the following:

Quality of products or services delivered

Quantity of good work or service produced

Timeliness of response to customer needs

Cost of work processes

If you cannot point to measurable improvement in one of these four areas, you don't have a TQM program or a reengineering program. You *may* have sloganeering and posters and training and buzzwords, but you don't have the thing itself.

Some organizations have built too large a quality apparatus. Quality has become its own administration with its own vice president and permanent staff. "They" are the group responsible for quality. That was never the objective in the original quality programs. Instead, quality must be driven by employees and line managers who integrate concepts of quality into the day-to-day work processes. The goal is not to build a great quality program. It is to use proven quality processes to build a great organization.

Karl Albrecht makes this point well:

> Quality as a thing unto itself is no longer the answer. It was a transition stage in our learning process. The focus [should not be] on quality, but on business success. This view will not endear me to some in the quality brotherhood (or the sisterhood), but we must face the truth of our circumstances.[3]

I once participated on a panel with Fred Smith, the founder and CEO of Federal Express. A conference participant asked him to describe the main features of the company's Total Quality Management program. His reply was simple: "We don't have one. We don't intend to *have* a total quality program; we intend to *be* a total quality company." Indeed, Fred Smith and his team set out from day one to build quality processes into his organization in such a way that it would affect everything they did. He succeeded magnificently. (In fairness, I should say that this is easier to do in a new organization than in an existing one. In an established company, TQM may have to be a program before it becomes a process.)

When TQM works, it passes through three phases. First, it is, in fact, a program (oriented mainly to training). Then it becomes a process, the way the company solves problems and improves operations. Finally, it becomes a passion. People throughout the organization become deeply committed to excellence and continuous improvement of all operations. The company or organization becomes obsessed with the customer, the person served. When it becomes a passion, it's finally real.

C. Jackson Grayson, chairman of The American Productivity and Quality Center, says that quality programs must be "in the heart and gut" before they can really produce anything. They must be "what the Japanese call 'an attitude of mind' or 'a way of life.'"[4]

If that is not yet true of your organization then that is the first problem you need to pinpoint and set out to solve. The next step in solving the problem is to do a thorough job of analyzing it. Chapter 8 will give you some practical tools for doing just that.

REFERENCES

1. Richard S. Johnson and Lawrence A. Kazense, *TQM: Mechanics of Quality Processes* (Milwaukee: ASQC Quality), 159.
2. Aubrey C. Daniels and Theodore A. Rosen, *Performance Management: Improving Quality and Productivity Through Positive Reinforcement* (Tucker, Ga.: Performance Management, 1983), 135–42.
3. Karl Albrecht, quoted in Scott Madison Patow, "New Gurus: The Next Leaders of the Quality Revolution," *Quality Digest*, March 1995, 38.
4. C. Jackson Grayson, quoted in "New Gurus: The Next Leaders of the Quality Revolution," 31.

8

THE PROCESS

◼

Removing Barriers to the Inner Spirit

Charles Steinmetz was one of M.I.T's most brilliant graduates, no small achievement for a man who struggled with the disability of being a dwarf. He was also the person who designed and constructed the original assembly line used by Henry Ford in his manufacturing plant in Detroit.

After the plant had been running for several years, the assembly line process developed quirks and problems that needed to be addressed. Ford, one of the richest people in the world, was also very tight with a buck. He tried to use engineers of lesser skill than Steinmetz to save money. These cheaper people only made matters worse. Finally, Ford realized he had to go for the best, the great engineer Charles Steinmetz.

Steinmetz arrived at the plant, rolled up his sleeves, and began tinkering with this, that, and the other thing. Within a few days he had that assembly line running like a top. He sent Henry Ford a bill for ten thousand dollars. In those days that amount of money would buy the nicest home in town. Ford was outraged. He fired off a letter to Steinmetz protesting that ten thousand dollars was too much money "for just tinkering around." He demanded that Steinmetz send him an itemized breakdown of his bill.

Charles Steinmetz replied in a famous letter, which can still be seen in the Henry Ford Museum in Dearborn, Michigan.

Dear Henry:

Here is the itemized breakdown of my bill which you requested:

For "tinkering around". . . . . $ 10.00
For knowing where to "tinker around" . . $ 9,990.00

Respectfully submitted,

Your Friend, Charlie

Henry Ford paid the bill.

Though his letter was brash, Charles Steinmetz made an excellent point. Anyone can tinker around with a process or "reengineer" an organization. That's a no-brainer. The challenge is to know where to tinker, to know how to reengineer so that the new process produces a better value for the customer.

This results from good analytical skills. Fortunately, problem analysis doesn't require a genius. It requires patience and following a disciplined procedure to reach the right conclusion.

You may have heard the story of a young child who drew all of his pictures in black. The teacher became concerned; then the parents became concerned. So they brought in the school psychologist. When the psychologist met with the child and asked him about his black pictures, the child responded, "Black is the only color crayon I have."

We often jump to the wrong conclusion because we do not take the time to analyze the situation and collect data. The result is that hours are spent trying to solve the wrong problem.

A hi-tech manufacturing process called "thin film" put layers of material on a substrate in order to make computer chips. The requirements for manufacturing necessitated a clean room environment. That meant special covering for clothes, no makeup, and strict sanitation procedures. The training department had a very good training program on clean room procedures. Each employee working in the clean room was required to go through the training.

But every few weeks the training department would get a call from management that the employees in the clean room were

THE PROCESS: *Removing Barriers to the Inner*

not following the clean room procedures. The train.
ment retrained everyone. And so the cycle went until
ing department head, knowing that his training pro;
sound, decided to take a look at what was going on.

Here is what he found. Senior management people were
going into the clean room without protective covering and pick-
ing up substrates with bare hands. Basically, they were operating
as if they were exempt from the clean room standards. After a
while, the employees began to follow the example of top management, not the teaching of the training department.

A college dean was frustrated because he did not have the
resources to hire the additional support staff he thought he
needed. In order to understand the situation more clearly, the
manager decided to observe the behavior of his employees on a
regular basis throughout the day. He noted when they were
engaged in productive work and when they were not. At the end
of the day the manager was astounded at the amount of time his
staff was not engaged in productive work. The problem was not
that he had too few employees. He could have hired several new
employees, and the real problem would have persisted.

A sales and marketing manager from a major glass manufacturing operation was frequently interrupted during the day by
phone calls. He tracked the number of calls and where they
were coming from and found that the majority were from his
own sales representatives. Some of them were even calling him
several times a day for guidance. The source of the problem was
not so much a time management issue as it was an empowerment issue. He set out to discover why his sales representatives
felt they needed to call so often and then assisted them in functioning more independently.

KNOWLEDGE—SKILL—ATTITUDE—SYSTEM

Problems in human performance are not an inscrutable mystery. In our PRIDE seminars we teach that all performance
problems fall into one of four categories:

1. *Knowledge.* Do the employees have enough information
   to know what they are to do?

2. *Skills.* Do the employees have the skills required to do the job?

3. *Attitude.* Do the employees have the attitudes that will enable them to do the job?

4. *System.* Do the employees find themselves frustrated by outdated, inappropriate systems?

Most human performance problems can be traced back to one of these four sources. Let's discuss them in order.

KNOWLEDGE PROBLEMS

A mistake we often make with employees is assuming that they have the knowledge they need. Sometimes employees don't have that knowledge and are tempted to fake it rather than admit they need help. This creates a vicious cycle between employee and management.

Most corporations in this country greatly underestimate the training task. In Japan it is not unusual to spend six weeks a year in formalized training. New recruits often spend six months to a year before being allowed to make products or have direct contact with customers.

SKILL PROBLEMS

To move from knowledge to skill requires practice—supervised practice. It is unlikely that a person will improve simply by experience. In fact, experience is highly overrated. Have you seen an improvement in your handwriting over the last fifteen years? Has your driving improved? Do marriages automatically get better? The truth is, if we do something over and over again we may start leaving out important parts. We often become less effective. Practice doesn't make perfect; it makes permanent.

The caddie at our golf club told me the other day, "Dr. Stevenin, I've been a caddie here for seven years, but you took me places today I've never been before." He wasn't telling me that I lacked knowledge, but that I lacked skill. How do I get skill? By playing a lot of golf? No. That is how I got so bad. If I really wanted to make this a priority in my life, I would have to practice with a pro who could give me corrective feedback.

Skills can go downhill. Many college presidents need to visit their own classrooms. They'd be astonished to see how the Outstanding Teacher of ten years ago is actually performing today. Sales managers need to accompany their veteran sales representatives on calls. They might be astonished. Salespeople can get lazy. They quit doing the very things that made them successful.

ATTITUDE PROBLEMS

The solution to attitude problems is changing the consequences. For years in this country, we said that as soon as people changed their attitudes about minorities and females, they would change their behavior. So we tried to educate people to change their attitudes.

How well did that work? It didn't work at all. Then the federal government came along and changed the consequences. It became illegal to discriminate on the basis of race or sex, and stiff penalties for doing so were established. We have been on that program for some thirty or forty years, and it is a long way from perfect. It's been a bumpy ride, to be sure. But the most profound sociological change going on in the United States today is probably the fundamental shift in attitudes about race and gender. That is a direct result of changing the consequences.

Attitude is paramount. One can possess the knowledge, the skill, and the systems for improving performance but fail in reaching goals because of poor attitudes and negative thinking. I spent the early part of my corporate career training a large sales force. Some people are convinced they can sell. Some people are convinced they cannot sell—anything, ever. The problem is that whichever they believe, they're right.

There is a new theory in hiring: Above all, hire people with good attitudes. Why? Because you can give people knowledge and teach them a skill, but you cannot necessarily give them the right attitude. Consequences can help, but they are no guarantee. The individual finally chooses his or her own attitude.

SYSTEM PROBLEMS

Employees may have excellent knowledge, skills, and attitudes but are still not getting results. This is usually a sign of a system problem.

A major manufacturer of farm equipment in the Midwest was having a difficult time keeping the necessary parts on hand. The organization had a computerized materials management system for tracking and reordering parts. However, the old-line managers relied instead on an ad hoc system they had been using for years. Every day each manager compiled a handwritten hot list based on a visible counting of parts. With hot lists in hand, management people met daily to review shortages and take necessary action to get the parts required. The hot list system was outdated and time-consuming. As long as it was in place it prevented an efficient operation from developing. The company had a computerized, simple alternative. All they had to do was use it.

W. Edwards Deming believed that 85 percent of all performance problems were system problems. That led to his work in reengineering, discussed elsewhere in this book.

DETERMINING THE ROOT PROBLEM

In determining whether our root problem is knowledge, skill, attitude, or system, we must gather data and study it. Let's review some of the most popular ways to gather and analyze data.

Interviews

One way to understand what is going on is to *conduct interviews*, simply talking to the people doing the work. Employees have the solutions to many of the problems within their work areas and sometimes within the whole organization. They are usually willing to assist with the solutions. But they need to be asked. Their information must be respected. They need to see evidence that their input is being acted upon. When our firm conducts interviews with employees, they are always cooperative and pleased that someone is finally asking their opinion.

Time Logs

It can be difficult for a manager to identify and know what should be going on because she or he is so busy just getting through the day and putting out fires. If this is the situation, it may be necessary to have employees keep track of their behaviors during the day in order to collect the data necessary for analysis and problem solving.

Looking at Existing Data

Most organizations have collected volumes of data and information but have never taken the time to analyze it and use it to implement improvements.

By analyzing the data on use of motor vehicles and establishing motor pools, one of our clients was able to reduce the number of vehicles necessary to carry out the work of the operation. The savings to the organization were sizable, and the remaining vehicles were kept in better condition.

Questionnaires and Surveys

These can be an effective and efficient way to gather information from large numbers of people in multiple locations. The information can be compiled to provide a picture of how situations are perceived by different people throughout the organization. Anonymity must be protected if the feedback is to be candid.

Cause-Effect Diagrams

Also called "fishbones," these charts are easy to understand and use. The technique uncovers the root cause of problems. It does just what it says. It pictures the possible causes and effects of a problem. The charts can be developed during a brainstorming session, and they provide good road maps for problem solving.

Barrier Analysis

This technique looks at potential hazards and how they might cause harm or incur damage. It also examines impediments. It is a way to determine the root cause of a problem or unwanted event by assessing safeguards that should have prevented the occurrence. Barrier analysis defines the basic elements of an unwanted event or problem.

Change Analysis

This technique systematically examines the effects of change. Change analysis can be effective in troubleshooting. For example, you may want to look at why competent individuals are not accomplishing what needs to be done when they formerly did so. What has changed?

Work Flow Diagrams

When operations flow from one department to another it is helpful to do a work flow chart so that you have a visual picture of what is actually going on. The truth revealed by flow charting is often quite different from what people think is going on. The technique is also called process analysis.

Flow charting can create a greater understanding and appreciation of what each worker contributes to the job. By drawing a flow chart, a client company was able to discover the tremendous amount of time required to develop the specifications and requirements for frequently occurring jobs. The chart depicted the repetitive steps used to visit the job site and write specifications, and it provided the information needed to cut out unnecessary work.

To develop a flow chart, list the activities as they are intended to occur. Then list what actually does occur. From these lists you can diagram the steps so that they are visibly obvious.

Dianne Galloway, in *Mapping Work Processes*, cites the benefits of mapping processes as useful to planning and creating new processes. Mapping provides a way to construct macro/micro processes. As a job aid, it helps to identify bottlenecks and inefficiencies, improves cycle time, and identifies steps that can be taken more efficiently by someone else.

Galloway identifies eight steps in the mapping process:

- State the outputs of the process.
- List the customers for your output.
- List the customer requirements for the output.
- List the process participants.
- List the process owners.
- List the stakeholders.
- Agree on the process boundaries, where you start and where you end.
- List inputs and their suppliers.[1]

Process reengineering is concerned with efficiency in time, money, and resources. It is concerned with how well the process accomplishes its purpose as seen by the customer. Process reengineering is called for when your current processes will not keep you competitive or move you ahead as quickly as you want. Lon Roberts, in *Process Reengineering: The Key to Achieving Breakthrough Success*, sees process reengineering and the continuous improvement process as complementary.[2] It may be necessary for an organization to redesign its processes quickly and radically; but after the redesign, those processes will need to be continually improved, for business processes tend to become inefficient over time.

Dean Spitzer, of the College of Education at Boise State University, developed a work improvement form designed to identify weaknesses in job design. The form looks at major questions in work design, focusing on effectiveness.

1. Does the task accomplish what it is supposed to accomplish?
2. Are there steps that could be eliminated or consolidated?
3. Are the work processes creating unnecessary delays?
4. Do workers see the results of their efforts?

5. Is the task being accomplished at the right pace?
6. What input and control do the employees have over the processes?
7. Are the purpose and context of the task clear?
8. What variety exists in the process that would motivate the employee?
9. Are there work flow problems from one area to another?
10. Is the work fairly distributed among employees?
11. Do workers receive feedback on how well they are doing?
12. Are the mechanized work systems adequately designed for operation?
13. Is there adequate documentation to assist employees in doing the job right the first time?
14. How adequate is the training?[3]

Spitzer has found these questions to be very effective in carrying out work-improvement efforts. The answers to these questions can help employees and management focus more objectively on solving performance problems.

During the analysis and information-gathering phases of problem solving, a clear picture should emerge as to the optimal performance expected, the actual performance taking place, the various feelings surrounding the situation, identification of cause(s) of the problem, and solutions based on factual data. If these areas are covered, you can be confident that realistic and workable solutions will emerge.

SELECT THE BEST SOLUTION

Once you have done the best analysis you can, you must choose the best solution. This is a critical point in the problem-solving process. This decision needs to be made well in order to proceed toward a solution. Decision making can be impeded by a variety of errors.

Russo and Schoemaker, in *Decision Traps: The Ten Barriers to Brilliant Decision-Making and How to Overcome Them*, list ten decision-making traps to avoid.

1. Plunging in without data
2. Framing the problem incorrectly
3. Failing to frame the problem in more than one way
4. Overconfidence in your judgment
5. Shortsighted shortcuts
6. Shooting from the hip
7. Groupthink
8. Fooling yourself about feedback
9. Not keeping track
10. Not auditing your own decision-making process[4]

Let's describe these traps in greater detail.

Plunging. Beginning to gather information and taking action without carefully considering the crux of the issue.

Frame blindness. Setting out to solve the wrong problem because you have already created a mental framework for your decision.

Lack of frame control. Failing to consciously define the problem in more than one way and being unduly influenced by the frames of others. This is an area in which a cross-functional team can make a significant contribution, because team members represent different perspectives. This can result in better decision making. Even insurance companies, notoriously careful in spending, encourage and pay for getting a second, and sometimes a third, medical opinion before authorizing surgery.

In Kansas City, Henry Block, a cancer survivor, helped establish a review board for cancer patients. The board was made up of representatives from various medical disciplines who came together to review individual cases. Block believed that patients would receive the best recommendations if the recommendations were prepared collectively by a team of experts who saw the problem from different perspectives.

Overconfidence in your judgment. Failing to look at and consider pertinent information because you are so sure about your assumptions and opinions. This is most dangerous when coupled with arrogance. An arrogant leader is often wrong but never in doubt.

The top management of IBM was convinced that the company's mainframe computer business could withstand the inroads of the personal computer. They were wrong. As a result, IBM lost a huge amount of business to young, upstart manufacturers. The company finally changed directions and managed to recover part of the lost market share. It is important to recognize what you don't know and what the risks are if your judgment turns out to be wrong.

Shortsighted shortcuts. Relying inappropriately on "rules of thumb," such as implicitly trusting the most readily available information. This often occurs when you are paying too much attention to current problems while ignoring hidden sources of future problems.

A technique called *fault trees* can be used to reveal potential obstacles. Fault trees are developed from brainstorming and from listing potential obstacles. This technique alerts you to potential problems and puts you in a position to take preventive measures.

Shooting from the hip. This amounts to believing you can keep mental track of all the information you've discovered and winging it rather than developing a systematic procedure with which to make your decisions. Intuition should sometimes be followed, but it shouldn't be the only decision-making method.

Groupthink. This occurs when you assume that with many smart people involved, good choices will automatically follow. Team decisions in the wrong environment can be disastrous. A prime example is the powerful team President John F. Kennedy assembled to make decisions concerning the Bay of Pigs. The result was a disaster.

Here are some common elements in destructive groupthink: Too much cohesiveness, insulation, high stress, and strong directive leadership. To counteract groupthink the leader must provide an atmosphere where the team does its work without undue influence from the leader, where new ideas are encouraged, and where personal criticism is discouraged.

Fooling yourself about feedback. Not accurately interpreting the information from past outcomes. One can learn from past mistakes if they are acknowledged and correctly interpreted. There is a real temptation to take credit for those things that went well and ignore the lessons of past failures.

Not keeping track. Assuming that experience will automatically bring enlightenment. It is important that you maintain an ongoing evaluation process, so that you are asking questions about what you are learning, the way you gather information, and the way you make decisions.

Not auditing your decision-making process. Here the fault lies in failing to evaluate your processes constantly, as well as where and how you spend your time. Throughout the criteria for the Malcolm Baldrige Quality Award there is a focus on how processes and procedures are evaluated. You cannot ask these questions too many times.

In our seminars, I sometimes divide the class in half and ask each group different questions. I give this question to group A:

You are buying an item in a retail store for $90. You know this identical item can be purchased in a store five blocks away for $40. Would you walk five blocks to the other store to get the lower price?

I distribute this question to Group B:

You are buying an item in a retail store for $9,990. You know that this identical item can be purchased in a store five blocks away for $9,940. Would you walk five blocks to the other store to get the lower price?

Virtually all members of Group A will opt to walk five blocks to get the lower price, but only a small minority of Group B will opt to walk five blocks for the lower price. The real question is identical—would you walk five blocks to save $50?—but the framing of the question makes an enormous difference in how the question is answered.

Once you have chosen a solution, try it out and keep careful track of the results. Take time also to celebrate and reward improvement. Once your solution has been tested, absorb it into your continuous improvement process and find another problem to solve. When does it end? It never ends. That's the price of excellence.

The PRIDE approach to problem solving establishes explicit values and creates an environment of trust when management does what it says it will do. Respect is fostered and employees become excited about being part of the solution. But you have to have management commitment and leadership. If you haven't got that, you're in trouble, because management controls the consequences.

Kiichiro Toyoda, the founder of Toyota, once found himself needing to lay off one-quarter of the work force of the then infant company. The workers protested. The final decision was that Toyoda himself would resign and take responsibility for the disgrace of laying off workers. The lasting benefit of Toyoda's resignation was that all employees, including top management, saw themselves as equally accountable for the success of the endeavor. When I visited and studied Toyota's operation a few years ago, I could still sense the deep commitment to quality in all the workers.

Delta Airlines set a similar example several years ago when it needed to reduce its staff expense by one-third. Instead of firing a third of the force, the entire company, from the CEO to the clerks, agreed to take a one-third reduction in salary. When profits returned, the grateful employee team chipped in and bought the company a new airplane.

Contrast that with an all-too-common situation in America: Management provides poor leadership and gets a company in serious trouble. Hundreds of workers lose their jobs and often their homes and their self-respect. But top management's compensation is very little affected. If a takeover ensues, they may even be given huge retirement settlements. In effect, they're being rewarded for incompetence. The workers have paid the price.

I once heard a brash executive of a large corporation ask W. Edwards Deming, the legendary quality guru, "Dr. Deming, what do you think I ought to do to get rid of all the deadwood I've got in my organization?" Deming, who was then ninety years of age, rocked back and forth and said nothing for several moments. Finally, he said, "I assume that you didn't hire any deadwood, so the real question is this: How, under your leadership, did so many people become deadwood? Sir, when you've answered that question, you'll know who needs to change."

REFERENCES

1. Dianne Galloway, *Mapping Work Processes* (Milwaukee, Wis.: ASQC Quality, 1994), 16–17.
2. Lon Roberts, *Process Reengineering: The Key to Achieving Breakthrough Success* (Milwaukee, Wis.: ASQC Quality, 1994).
3. Dean R. Spitzer, "Performance Improvement Ideas," *Performance and Instruction*, April 1988, 40–41.
4. J. Edward Russo and Paul J. Schoemaker, *Decision Traps: The Ten Barriers to Brilliant Decision-Making and How to Avoid Them* (New York: Doubleday, 1989), 159.

9

THE PLAN

◪

Giving Direction to the Inner Spirit

In organizations you will generally find three kinds of people:

Those who make things happen.
Those who watch things happen.
Those who didn't know anything was happening.

Those who make the right things happen at a high level of excellence are the key to the future. These are the people who do the right things right. But the only way you know the right things to do is if you have a clear vision of the future.

When we ask the leaders of a business or any other type of organization to tell us their greatest problem, invariably the answer comes back: "Communication!"

Like most simplistic answers, this one is wrong. Most people in organizations know how to communicate, want to communicate, and enjoy communicating (watch them at coffee break). The real problem in most organizations is that people don't know what to communicate about. They don't have a strategy, a game plan. They need to design their dream.

Russ Ackoff, in *Creating the Corporate Future*, identifies four approaches to strategic planning:

Reactive—
    This is planning by looking in the rearview mirror;
Inactive—
    Going with the flow;
Preactive—
    Planning for the future;
Proactive—
    Making your plan come true.[1]

Ackoff makes an interesting distinction between the *preactive* and the *proactive*. In preactive planning we're designing the strategy; in the proactive stage we're making it happen.

Plans are worthless. *Implemented plans* are priceless. It's like the story of the four birds:

> Four birds were sitting on a tree branch. One of them decided to fly away. Now how many birds were left on the branch?

The answer, of course, is that there were still four birds on the branch, because deciding to fly away and actually flying away are two different things. Deciding to diet may lead to frustration, but actually dieting leads to a healthier body. The difference is commitment and follow-through. You can't be like the kamikaze pilot who flew fifty-six missions!

Highly successful companies are self-critical and open to change. We in Missouri are extremely proud of a St. Louis-based corporation known as Wainwright Industries. In 1993, it received the Missouri Quality Award for excellence in manufacturing. In the process of winning this award it was examined by quality experts who prepared an extensive report on things done well and areas needing improvement. (Norma Boyer, a member of our consulting team, serves as Senior Examiner for the award.)

After Wainwright won the award, did it rest on its laurels? No. It took the feedback report from the state examining team and used it to develop and implement an improvement strategy for every area of the company. No wonder that, in 1994, the company won the Malcolm Baldrige National Quality Award, the nation's highest award for quality. At Wainwright Industries, they understand that good enough is not good enough.

John P. Kotter, professor of leadership at Harvard Business School, cites eight steps for making a corporate strategy for change and improvement really work:

1. Establishing a sense of urgency
2. Forming a powerful guiding coalition
3. Creating a vision to direct the change effort
4. Communicating the vision
5. Empowering others to act on the vision
6. Planning for visible improvements and rewarding those involved
7. Consolidating improvements and invigorating the process
8. Institutionalizing the new approaches[2]

In our planning with major corporations and nonprofit organizations, my company emphasizes that there are four elements in designing the future of an organization:

Our Mission	Why do we exist?
Our Goals	What do we want to accomplish?
Our Plan	How are we going to do it?
Our Budget	What is the projected income and expense of the plan?

These four elements add up to the vision, for the vision and the mission of a company are the same.

THE MISSION STATEMENT

A mission statement provides boundaries, clarifies what a company is attempting to do, helps form the culture, improves communication inside and outside the organization, and gives a basis for making decisions.

The mission statement needs to include *what* the organization does, *who* the customers are, *what* the organization produces, and *what* the organization values. Let's look at some well-known mission statements, or parts of those statements.

Quality, Service, Cleanliness, Value.

Whose mission statement is this?
Answer: McDonald's Restaurants®
Has this mission statement contributed to the company's success?

Here's part of a very different kind of mission statement:

*We believe our first responsibility is to people,
not profits, to patients, to parents, to doctors and nurses
and all human beings who use our product.*

Whose mission statement is this?
Answer: Johnson & Johnson Pharmaceuticals

Remember when this mission statement helped Johnson & Johnson make a critical decision? A trial by fire for Johnson & Johnson's stated mission was the 1982 Tylenol® crisis. A madman had put cyanide in some Tylenol capsules and killed five people. The entire organization mobilized within hours to recall all Tylenol in the distribution chain, nationwide. It cost the firm a billion dollars. Only two more contaminated pills were ever found.

Immediately after the tampering, a survey found that half of all Tylenol users said they would never buy the product again, but by 1985, the company had recovered almost all of its 35 percent share of the analgesic market.

Here's another short mission statement:

Quality is Job One.

Whose statement is this?
Answer: Ford®

Actually, this is a shortened version of a longer mission statement, but it captures the essence of Ford's mission. Have you noticed how many mission statements are finding their way into advertising? Good organizations want to tell you what they're all about.

How important has Ford's renewed sense of mission been to the company? The Taurus® was the first car in America designed, produced, and marketed entirely by employee quality teams. Even after the car hit the market, the quality teams contributed an additional seven hundred ideas for making it better or selling it more effectively. Ford estimates that the average value of each idea was $700,000.

Taurus was the most successful American car of the 1980s. In January 1993, it became the first American-made car in two decades to outsell Honda®. General Motors® is now attempting to do the same thing with Saturn®.

PITFALLS IN CREATING MISSION STATEMENTS

Stay away from crafting the words of the mission too much. Make sure the statement evokes feeling and passion. The statement should say who you are and why you're passionate about it. Aim for a broad focus on the spirit of what you do. Make the statement short—try not to have more than three sentences.

A mission statement evokes a personal response. Work on the statement until it is so clear that reminding yourself of it on a really bad day will keep you from walking out the door.

Don't mistake a slogan for a mission statement. A slogan may be something like:

Just Do It
The Best Way
One for All
A Thousand More by 2004

Slogans focus attention, but they don't communicate a sense of the purpose of the organization, nor do they have the enduring power of a mission statement.

Inspiring visions are not about numbers, growth, or investment. People become enthusiastic about being the best, producing goods or services that are of the highest quality or are the most innovative. Include enough stretch in your vision statement that it will be a challenge and a reason for working together.

Here are some questions I like to ask when I'm directing a planning retreat for a leadership team.

- If we had the organization of our dreams, what would it be like?
- If we could be what we wanted in five years, what would we be?
- How would we know we were there?
- What would be a stretch for ourselves?
- What kind of leadership team do we want to be?
- What do we really want to do or create?
- What would be worth committing to over the next ten years?
- How do we differentiate ourselves from other organizations?
- Does our mission motivate, inspire, and bring out the best in people?

A powerful mission statement:

- Presents where we want to go
- Is easy to read and understand
- Captures the desired spirit of the organization
- Is dynamically incomplete so that people can fill in the pieces
- Is compact and can be used to guide decision making
- Gets people's attention
- Describes a preferred and meaningful future state
- Can be felt and experienced and gives people goose bumps when they hear it
- Gives people a better understanding of how their individual purpose can be realized in the group

- Provides a motivating force, even in hard times
- Is perceived as achievable
- Is challenging and compelling, stretching beyond what is comfortable

CORE VALUES

Mission statements sometimes include a section on general strategies or core values. Sometimes these two things are woven together. For several years we worked closely with a restaurant company headquartered in Kansas City. Here is their mission statement, followed by ten core values:

Mission Statement
We are committed to being a profitable, dynamic, growing business organization focused on making every guest a repeat guest.

Core Values
1. *We will be an innovator in our industry in such areas as menu development, food creations, guest services and restaurant environment.*
2. *We will treat each other with fairness and respect, and with the same courtesy and consideration that we seek to achieve in the treatment of our guests.*
3. *We will foster an atmosphere of open, honest, two-way communication by carefully listening to our employees and our guests.*
4. *We will empower employees at all levels with the authority to take whatever actions are necessary to achieve our mission.*
5. *We will create a corporate environment which provides for and promotes the personal and professional growth of all employees.*
6. *We will recognize and reward all employees based on their contribution to the achievement of our mission, goals and plans.*

7. *We will follow a carefully planned, disciplined approach to expansion and growth.*
8. *We will be a respected and responsible member of the communities we serve.*
9. *We will conduct ourselves in accordance with the highest standards of business ethics.*
10. *We will continually improve our organization and all of its operations.*

In *The Power of Vision*, George Barna urges churches to carefully state the purpose for their ministry and then to ask the following questions about it.

- If someone contacted your church regarding involvement in what seemed like a reasonable ministry opportunity, is the [vision] statement specific enough to permit you to have a ministry-oriented reason to reject that opportunity and to explain the reasoning for the rejection?
- Does the statement include information which, when compared to the vision statements of nearby churches, clearly sets your church apart in a significant manner?
- Is the statement one that points the ministry in a clear and unique direction for the future?
- Does the statement lead to a precise understanding regarding the strategies and tactics that are permissible in ministry?
- Does the statement provide focus for the ministry so that people are excited about being involved in the work of the church?
- Does the statement prevent the church from seeking to be all things to all people?
- Have any inactive Christians who regularly attend the church become excited about the prospects for ministry after being exposed to this statement?[3]

Some long-established organizations have mission statements that are badly out-of-date or use overly formal, stilted language. Look at the following examples to see how reworking the mission statement of an organization gives it more energy.

The Sierra Club

Before: *The mission of the Sierra Club is to influence public, private and corporate policies and actions through Club programs at the local, national and international levels.*

After: *Building on generations of success, the Sierra Club inspires people to join in protecting earth's natural treasures and vitality. Through the club, individuals magnify their power to restore the places where they live and preserve the places they love.*

Union School District

Before: *The Union School District is dedicated to serving the educational needs of pupils within the community. The board of trustees, staff members and the state share in the responsibilities for the education of pupils. The commitment is to provide a free public education to maintain a literate populace, which is the basis for a democratic society.*

After: *In Union District, we are committed to providing the necessary resources and inspiration for each student to develop a command of learning, social responsibility and critical thinking. We are dedicated to motivating students to achieve their maximum potential and to value lifelong learning.*

Steven R. Covey, in *The Seven Habits of Highly Effective People*, lists as his second habit "Begin with the end in mind."[4] Covey emphasizes the principle that all things are created twice. First is the mental image of creation, and then there is the physical creation.

Once, as I walked about the impressive grounds of Disney University in California, I said to a colleague, "Isn't it a shame that Walt Disney didn't live long enough to see this all take place?" On the flight home I realized what a dumb comment that was. Of course, he *did* live long enough to see it. He envisioned the whole incredible, unlikely, imaginative thing and probably in great detail. He was a visionary. He communicated that vision in a powerful way to his colleagues before his death. He saw it all.

THE GOALS

Suppose I came to your organization tomorrow and asked the first person who came down the hall, "What would you say is the single most important goal this organization is trying to accomplish right now?" What would the answer be? If people can't answer that question, they don't even know which direction they are going.

Measurable goals are important because they tell the employee precisely what is expected. Ferdinand F. Fournies, in *Why Employees Don't Do What They're Supposed to Do*, says,

> As amazing as this may sound, the most common reason managers give as to why people at work don't do what they are supposed to do is "They don't know what they are supposed to do." At its worst, this means literally that people do not know there is a specific task they should perform. Variations of this problem are:
>
> - They know they are supposed to do something, but they don't know when they are supposed to begin.
> - They know they are supposed to do something and know when they are supposed to begin, but they don't know when they are supposed to finish.
> - They know what to do, when to begin it, and when to end it, but they don't know what finished is supposed to look like. You told them to do a good job, but they don't know whether a good job is ten percent error, five percent error, or error-free performance.[5]

The world's greatest archer is so good he can hit the target dead center. But you could set up a situation in which anyone could beat him. All you would have to do is blindfold him. Now, that doesn't seem fair. You're right, it isn't. But I spend probably half my time as a consultant trying to get leaders to understand that people cannot hit a target they cannot see. Nor can they hit a target that doesn't exist. If you don't know where you want to go, any road will get you there.

A smart goal must be clear and understandably specific about what it will achieve, and it must reflect a belief that the goal is worthwhile. Larson and LaFasto, in *Teamwork: What Can Go Wrong, What Must Go Right*, say:

> Clarity implies that there is a specific performance objective, phrased in such concrete language that it is possible to tell, unequivocally, whether or not that performance objective has been attained.[6]

In other words, there is a clear "Go/No Go Test" for attainment.

John F. Kennedy said, "At the end of this decade we will put a man on the moon and return him safely to the earth." This clearly focused goal propelled NASA into the finest space exploration effort in the world. What if Kennedy had challenged NASA simply to be an excellent, world-class space exploration agency and nothing more? It would still be designing the launch pad.

Goals define the end results the organization wants to achieve in a given time frame. There are significant differences between a mission and a goal.

MISSION	GOALS
Broad, General	Specific
Not Quantifiable	Nearly Always Quantifiable
Unmeasurable	Measurable
No Time Frame	Definite Time Frame
No Deadline	Clear Deadline
Comprehensive	Priorities Only

> *A Good Way to Think of Goals*
>
> *Is That They Must Be*
>
> *SMART*
>
> *Specific*
>
> *Measurable*
>
> *Attainable*
>
> *Realistic*
>
> *Timely*

There are two excellent ways to fail in leadership:

1. Do an equally good job of everything (all things are not equally important).
2. Do an excellent job of the wrong thing!

Goals help us focus on priorities. Although all goals should be measurable, not all goals are numerically quantifiable. Some goals are measurable primarily in the sense that the deadline for "launch" or "arrival" is met.

Examples:

To start a campaign aimed at increasing store traffic from the nearby business complex no later than April 10.

To evaluate the current strengths and weaknesses of our company's design and appearance and to launch a cost-effective upgrade no later than June 30.

Note that it could be argued that neither of these statements is really a goal, but only outlines steps leading to a more important goal. That is true, but sometimes a project is so large in itself that it deserves the status of a goal.

Sometimes a goal is by its very nature difficult to measure.

Example:

To increase the level of trust and communication effectiveness among the management team members no later than December 30.

In this case we say a goal should be *recognizable* if not precisely *measurable*. In other words, you could recognize the difference in a management team where there is a high level of trust and good communication and one that lacks those qualities.

If we have a goal that is not measurable, we should have an extremely measurable plan. In other words, if a reasonable person followed that plan step by step, would he arrive at the goal? If so, the plan is a good application of strategic planning.

To summarize:

• Most goals should be quantifiable.
• Some goals are quantifiable only in terms of meeting the deadline.
• Some goals are more recognizable than measurable.
• The more unmeasurable the goal, the more measurable the plan must be.
• An unmeasurable goal supported by an unmeasurable plan is just gobbledegook.

Here is a good format for writing a goal:

Our goal is:

To have _____ _____
                      verb   *subject*

by _____ no later than _____
standard (number or percentage)   *deadline*

Here are some examples:

To have *increased sales over the previous year* by *18 percent* no later than *December 31.*

To have *reduced accounts receivable in relation to sales* by *9 percent* no later than *May 1 of this year.*

To have *increased the number of church members actively participating in small group fellowships* by *30 percent* no later than *June 15 of next year.*

To have *trained all mid-level managers in the PRIDE Quality Improvement Process* no later than *the end of the second quarter.*

THE ACTION PLAN

Each goal must be supported by a plan of action to achieve the goal. The *action plan* should answer the following questions:

- Which persons are to be involved?
- When? (Beginning when and accomplished when?)
- What resources are required?
- Are new forms or documentation required?
- How much will it cost?
- What training is needed?

An action plan need not list every possible element (set up chairs, turn on lights, plug in coffee, etc.). It should, however, list the major steps toward the goal. If the organization takes each one of those steps, it should arrive at the goal.

Action plans should specify key staff who will take the lead in getting the goal accomplished. A good practice is to have the first person listed be the one responsible for initiating the various steps. Plans should also estimate the budgetary requirements (if any) of the various steps in carrying out each action.

Here are two forms we use when we help organizations plan for the future.

PLANNING FORM A: ISSUES & ACTIONS PLANNING FORM B: GOALS AND ACTION PLANS

Planning Form A

Issues/Opportunities	Possible Actions
1.	1.
2.	2.
3.	3.
4.	4.
5.	5.
6.	6.
7.	7.
8.	8.
9.	9.
Goal:	

Note: Think of *issues* as barriers to achievement, chronic problems, or weaknesses in staff development. Think of *opportunities* as situations in the marketplace that could provide unique opportunities. Use this background discussion to formulate a goal and an action plan to solve the problem or seize the opportunity.

Planning Form B

STRATEGIC GOALS AND ACTION PLANS

GOALS AND ACTION PLANS	KEY PERSONS	DEADLINE	BUDGET REQUIREMENTS	PROGRESS REVIEW
Goal: To have (action) (subject) by (standard) no later than (deadline)				
Action Plan 1. *How?* 2. *Resources Required* 3. *Order of steps* 4. 5.	Who will do it. If a team is involved, the first person listed is the initiator or team leader.	List a deadline for the goal and each action step leading to the goal.	Specify budget implications, if any. This is not required if it has already been done in other documents.	Use this column to report to your supervisor each month on your progress.

In reviewing action plans, look for the following:

1. Are the steps clear? (Inexperienced planners will tend to simply write other goals into the action plan rather than actual steps for achievement.)
2. Do these action plan elements "have a handle?" Will people know what to take hold of and actually do?
3. Are important steps omitted?
4. Are time frames adequate? (We usually underestimate.)
5. Are key steps taken early enough in the year to get results this year?
6. Does each step have at least one name by it? As leaders, remember that anything not delegated is automatically assigned to you by default.

CONTINGENCY PLANNING

Anyone going to the trouble of developing an action plan will think it's nearly perfect. But what about a dose of humility? To avoid Murphy's Law, the best approach is contingency planning. Obstacles to successful implementation can be obvious or hidden. Use the *Contingency Planning Worksheet* to think through what could go wrong, what you can do to avoid it, and if worse comes to worst, how you will get out of the pickle.

CONTINGENCY PLANNING WORKSHEET

WHAT COULD GO WRONG?	HOW COULD YOU PREVENT IT FROM HAPPENING?	HOW WILL YOU FIX IT IF IT HAPPENS?

The book *Plan or Die!* lists ten keys to shaping your organization's future success:

1. Base decisions on values.
2. Have a mission based upon a shared vision.
3. Sound a rallying cry and persevere.
4. Promote and reward risk taking.
5. Empower people—all of the people.
6. Create and nurture a learning organization.
7. Encourage innovation and flexibility.
8. Monitor and manage "down board."
9. Maintain a market focus.
10. Conduct applied strategic planning.[7]

THE BUDGET

Once your action plan is in place, you can prepare a budget, a statement of the projected income and expense of the action plan. Note that it is the *action plan* that calls for expenditures and projects income. Not until you have a completed action plan will you be prepared to *budget*. Here are four impossible tasks:

1. To budget a goal
2. To create a budget with no plan
3. To carry out a plan without a budget
4. To carry out a plan you can't afford

A learning game called *Business Literacy* is a way to teach employees about the financial implications of the organization. The game takes the players through forecasting on the basis of the previous year's revenues and costs. As the game progresses, the results are tracked and graphed. The reality of forecasts against actual expenditures and income is presented, and the players must use analytical skills to see why they are off and how to make up the difference.

The game expands the knowledge of employees, helps

reduce their fear of numbers, and gives them a greater understanding of how their behavior and decisions impact the bottom line.

This approach to training employees is described in *The Power of Open-Book Management*, by John Schuster.

> The financial part of a business and the people in that business are inextricably linked. . . . But most of the involvement, quality and empowerment efforts of the past decade missed that key point. They separated the so-called "soft" people side of the business [from] the so-called "hard" financial know-how side of the business. The power of open-book management is bridging that gap. The power happens when people are engaged in the heart and soul and guts of the business. Open-book management plugs all the people of the business into a new power supply, business and financial information they can use to make daily decisions on the job. This allows them to release more of their potential, their heads and hands and hearts, while advancing the business toward its goals.[8]

Nonprofit organizations as well as businesses can use the concepts of open-book management. A church in North Carolina does its budgeting and planning process by department. When each department has submitted its plan and the budget required to support it, the complete package is presented to the congregation for review. The members are given the opportunity to pledge what they will give to support the programs. If the pledges do not support the budget, each department must make necessary cuts until the budget requirements are in line with the pledges. This process gives the congregation the opportunity to see exactly where their money will be used and the opportunity to see the effects of their giving on the programs for the coming year.

Here's a tip for anyone who has to raise money from the public to support humanitarian or service programs. Don't dwell on your budget; dwell on your dreams. People don't give sacrificially to budgets. They often give sacrificially to make a dream come true.

Do you want to be a leader? Dream dreams. Have visions. Define your ultimate purpose. Do these things well and employees will rally in support of the task. In the early days of the National Aeronautics and Space Administration, the local press came to interview employees. One of the persons interviewed was a janitor, who stated that his job was to help put a man on the moon. He was involved and energized by a mission that transformed his repetitive job into an achievement greater than what he alone could produce.

REFERENCES

1. Russell Lincoln Ackoff, *Creating the Corporate Future: Plan or Be Planned For* (New York: Wiley, 1981).
2. John P. Kotter, "Leading Change: Why Transformation Efforts Fail," *Harvard Business Review*, March-April 1995, 61.
3. Taken from George Barna, *The Power of Vision: How You Can Capture and Apply God's Vision for Your Ministry* (Ventura, Calif.: Regal, 1992), 40–41.
4. Steven R. Covey, *The Seven Habits of Highly Effective People* (New York: Simon & Schuster, 1989), 96ff.
5. Ferdinand F. Fournies, *Why Employees Don't Do What They're Supposed to Do and What to Do About It* (New York: McGraw-Hill, 1988), 13.
6. Carl E. Larson and Frank M. J. LaFasto, *Teamwork: What Can Go Wrong, What Must Go Right* (Newbury Park, Calif.: Sage, 1989), 8.
7. Timothy M. Nolan, Leonard D. Goodstein, and J. William Pfeiffer, *Plan or Die! Ten Keys to Organizational Success*, ed. Jo Ann Padgett (Amsterdam: Pfeiffer, 1993), 27.
8. John P. Schuster, *The Power of Open-Book Management* (New York: Wiley, 1996).

10

THE TEAM

◪

Setting the Inner Spirit on Fire

I'm a great believer in teams. Why? Because they work. Properly set up, teams can accomplish great things in organizational life. Here are just a few things I've personally seen teams accomplish:

- An automobile manufacturer saw rejects go from seven rejects per one hundred cars to six rejects per one thousand cars.
- A collection agency saw collections go from $3 million a month to $7 million a week.
- A credit union went from 50 IRAs per month to 250 IRAs per month.
- A mortgage banking company reduced a thirty-day loan-approval process to a to five-day loan approval process.
- A bank went from sixteen new customers per week to forty new customers per week.
- An inner-city school went from an average of thirty-five days missed per year per student to an average of eighteen days missed per year.
- A church went from a dwindling congregation of eighty-five to a growing congregation of four hundred.

- A manufacturer went from four hundred union grievances per year to no grievances for the past three years.

These are not achievements I've read about or heard about. They are achievements I've witnessed, lived, seen first-hand. You have to be there to know how exciting it can be. Not only have I seen situations transformed in the team process, I've seen some team members transformed.

- From chronic complainers to positive contributors
- From adversaries of management or union to team members, partners, and problem solvers
- From low self-esteem to a much higher sense of self-worth
- From shabby, sloppy dressers to sharp, businesslike professional-looking people
- From a feeling of despair to a feeling of efficacy and empowerment
- From suspicion to trust, the essential element in all human relationships

On the other hand, teams are no guarantee of success. They can easily fail, and their failure can dampen enthusiasm and chill the inner spirit. Make sure that when you introduce teams or quality circles they are part of a total quality culture that continuously improves all aspects of the work environment, rewards innovation, and gives emphasis to nurturing the inner spirit of the work force.

Drew Lathin says that it is "simplistic and absurd" to think that "design teams can literally start with a blank piece of paper and innovatively reengineer right from the very beginning." Instead, design teams need (1) "knowledge of the work process"; (2) "analysis [of] the organization's business environment, work process, and social system"; and (3) "analysis of the organizational culture." You need to know "why things are done as they are" so that you will be aware of which "aspects of the culture . . . are congruent . . . with work process changes you want to enact" and which are not.[1]

DANGEROUS ASSUMPTIONS ABOUT TEAMS

It is dangerous to call groups *teams* in the belief that team language alone will change the way work is done, or to pretend you no longer need managers or leaders. Team members need leaders to help set standards, plan the work, coach, and give feedback.

It is dangerous to assume that teams can develop on their own without strong, visible support from leadership, or to overlook the need teams have to be given a clear vision and for the company or organization to clarify what it expects of them.

It is also dangerous to assume that setting up teams is an isolated act, with few or no implications for systems or other functions in the organization, or to overlook the need to teach the skills that everyone will require for a successful transition.

TRADITIONAL, HIERARCHICAL SYSTEMS VERSUS TEAMS

Once a company truly converts to a team-based system of management, it suddenly discovers a whole new set of problems. Here are a few to be prepared for:

- The employees lack team skills. America is not a team culture (unlike Japan). It is a highly individualistic culture, and fast trackers, people who break out of the pack, or people who march to the beat of a different drummer are rewarded. People have to be trained to work as a team.
- The company motivates people by competition, not collaboration, and sees collaboration as weak and indecisive.
- The reward system hasn't yet caught up with the team concept. If a company really wants to foster teamwork, it must consider team recognition and reward.
- The larger system in the company is not team-oriented, even though teams may appear in the company. Job classifications, information systems, the roles of the supervisors, performance appraisal, compensation, and a dozen other things may be out-of-date.

If there are too many system incongruities, the team approach will collapse.

OUTSTANDING TEAMS

In one of the best books ever written on teamwork in business, government, and sports, the authors say that all great teams (1) have clear, elevating, and inspiring goals; (2) operate within a results-driven structure; (3) have competent team members; (4) have a unified commitment to a goal; (5) operate in a collaborative climate; (6) have high standards of excellence; (7) receive management support and recognition; and (8) have principled, moral, ethical leadership.[2]

Really great teams have a great atmosphere. They are exciting and intellectually stimulating. They nourish the inner spirit. Here is what makes for such a great team atmosphere.

1. **Mission:** The members clearly understand the purpose of the team and have agreed on an up-to-date mission statement.

2. **Commitment:** The members take the additional time and invest the extra effort needed to work together as a productive team.

3. **Goals:** Team goals are written in clear, specific, and measurable terms and are supported by all members.

4. **Action plans:** Each member knows what actions to take on a weekly and daily basis to implement the team's goals.

5. **Strengths:** The members recognize and appreciate each other's personality strengths and openly discuss any conflicts.

6. **Rules:** All members have been involved in establishing the rules and procedures that help them work well together.

7. **Roles:** The team has recently clarified and has jointly agreed upon the roles and responsibilities of each member.

8. **Problem solving:** All members understand and use procedures that keep discussions positive and solution-focused.

9. **Creativity:** The members discuss issues in a manner that enhances creativity and establishes an open, risk-taking climate.

10. **Decision making:** The members understand each other's different styles and use effective decision-making techniques.

11. **Meetings:** Team meetings have clear agendas and follow procedures that make them efficient and productive.

12. **Evaluation:** The members regularly discuss areas of teamwork that could be improved and create plans for change.

QUESTIONS ABOUT TEAMS

Can an existing department be a team? This one always surprises me. Of course, a department can be a team. It *must* be a team. It can't begin to function without the characteristics of a team.

When do you need a formal team? You need a team when you are trying to solve a problem that involves more than one department. A cross-functional problem requires a cross-functional solution. The existing departmental structure can't solve such problems.

Should teams be appointed or made up of volunteers? To the greatest extent possible, I like to see people on a team because they want to be. If the volunteer list lacks expertise, management may have to encourage others to participate so that the team will have the resources it needs.

Should team leaders be appointed or elected? I like to see the team choose its own leader. I know this scares some of my management colleagues. I also have seen some bad choices—but very few in thirty years. If a team is truly empowered, let it make its own first major decision. I have also seen some unlikely choices blossom into good leaders.

How long should a team function? Unless it is a massive

project, we suggest four to six months. During this time the team will follow a disciplined schedule of weekly meetings (ninety minutes) and make assignments to be carried out between meetings.

A good way to put a team together is to send out a letter inviting those interested to respond.

MEMORANDUM

TO: Department Staff
FROM: Management

DATE:

Re: Quality-Improvement Teams

We are embarking on a unique and exciting quality-improvement process at XYZ Corporation. We need your help and participation. If you would be interested in being a part of this quality experience, please indicate by signing up today for our quality-improvement team.

Requirements for participation are a willingness to try out some new ideas by using your creativity in problem solving and having an interest in making our company an even better place to work. You will be asked to look at one area for improvement, evaluate what is currently happening in that area, come up with ways to make improvements, and celebrate the success of working together.

Although we encourage your involvement in this first quality-improvement team, if you are not a part of this first team, there will be other opportunities in the near future. The management team at XYZ Corporation is excited and supportive of this quality initiative, and we are eager to get the ball rolling!

Thank you for your interest in working together in this exciting venture.

☐ *Yes, I'm interested in working on the first quality-improvement team.*

To get started, teams often need an outside facilitator or coach. This can be a professional consultant from the outside, although it can also be an internal person with special training and skills. If an internal person is used, he or she should not have a hidden agenda or be politically involved in the outcome. Once the team leader is chosen, the facilitator plays a behind-the-scenes role. The roles of the facilitator and the leader are very different.

Leading	Facilitating
Feedback on individual contribution	Feedback on team function
Guiding task performance	Observation of process
Guidance on problem solving	Guidance on teamwork
Setting objectives	Helping define goals
Selecting projects/problems	Assessing selection process
Supporting individuals	Supporting the team
Leading meetings	Observing what goes on in meetings
Challenging the team	Challenging the process

TEAM CHAMPIONS

A team also needs to have a senior manager as its primary contact person. This executive should meet with the team early on to discuss the problem to be solved, indicate the resources that can be used, specify parameters, and clarify expectations. Then the manager should get out of the way, returning when requested, and let the team function. The executive serves as a link to the rest of the organization, championing the team's importance, running political interference, and reviewing the final recommendations before they're presented.

Teams should not be totally self-directed. Make clear the limits of authority, but give the team full freedom within those limits. Don't intervene unnecessarily in the process. Let the team process work: let the inner spirit come alive. You may be astounded at the results.

TEAM RESPONSIBILITIES

Team members should have a realistic understanding of their roles and accountabilities. They should demonstrate objective and fact-based judgments and collaborate effectively with other team members. They should make the goal of the team a higher priority than any personal objective, demonstrate a willingness to devote whatever effort is necessary to achieve the team's success, and be willing to share information, perceptions, and feedback openly.

Team members should help others on the team when it is needed and appropriate, and they should demonstrate high standards of excellence. They should get behind and support the team's decisions, demonstrate the courage of their convictions by directly confronting important issues, demonstrate leadership in ways that contribute to the team's success, and respond constructively to feedback from others.

Team leaders should set boundaries, interpret company goals, and help the team set its own goals. They should evaluate and track the team's progress toward its goals, ask questions, listen, show understanding, and summarize. They should seek divergent viewpoints, record ideas, use group-process techniques (such as brainstorming, problem solving, and prioritization), ask questions, listen, seek common interests, and summarize.

Team leaders should confront in a constructive way, give clear directions, intervene to keep the group on track, "read" the group and make adjustments where necessary, remain neutral (if possible), and suggest alternative processes to help the group achieve its goal.

TEAM RULES

Some teams have found that conflict can be lessened by determining clear team rules. Here is one team's list of rules:

Rule One. We will always be on time for meetings—right on time. If we must be late or absent, we will inform the team leader or a team member at least a day in advance.

Rule Two. We will always come to meetings prepared to work on the agenda we received before the meeting. Our preparation and data collection will be complete, and we will be ready to discuss the issues on the agenda.

Rule Three. We will always respect the opinions and feelings of all individuals. Each member has equal participation in our meetings. When discussing team business, members should expect to contribute to the discussions and to be listened to with respect.

Rule Four. We will always avoid blaming people for the short-comings of our team. If our team somehow fails to do its tasks properly, we will examine our team process and attempt to improve it. If individuals are having trouble meeting their commitments, the team will support them in every way possible.

Rule Five. Members will support the decisions of the team after they are made. Undermining team decisions or second-guessing and bad-mouthing the team and its work outside the team setting to nonmembers are *unacceptable* behaviors.

Rule Six. Members will live up to their team commitments, recognizing that failure to do so affects the whole team's progress. When in jeopardy of not meeting an obligation, the team member will notify the team in time for other members to take supportive action.

Rule Seven. When faced with a decision, we will first decide *how* to make the decision. Our general rule is to (1) state the problem, (2) discuss different ideas, (3) examine the benefits and risks associated with different approaches, and (4) select an approach we can all support. Other methods may also be appropriate.

Rule Eight. We will deal with conflict in a productive way. Our general rule for conflict is to understand the problem as best we can from each side's perspective. To do that, we will listen to all sides of the conflict, looking for facts and evidence. If there is still a conflict about facts, we will gather additional data. When the problem is understood, the team will help those in conflict create alternative approaches. If misunderstandings are not corrected through this approach, we will call a special meeting to address the conflict.

A team exists to solve a problem. Through analysis, the team will discover why something is a problem, which will in turn lead to an effective solution. Long-term solutions to problems require that problems be thoroughly analyzed, not just given a glance. For tips on analyzing and solving problems, see other chapters in this book.

SOURCES OF INFORMATION

Information currently available will include the collective information the team members bring with them, information from other company associates, information from customers, and data available from such sources as accounting reports, computer reports on customers, and reports on work processes.

The team may need to gather other information or carry out research. It must determine the data it needs to gather, how that information should be gathered, how long it needs to be gathered, who will gather it, who will analyze it, how the data will be presented, and how the data will be used to make decisions.

Part of gathering data may be for team members simply to go out and observe their associates. The objective is to find out how things are done now. When this approach is used, the following procedure is important:

THE TEAM: *Setting the Inner Spirit on Fire* ◼ 161

1. Determine the specific data required.
2. Determine the best way to do observations.
3. Review your plan for observation with management to gain support.
4. Meet with the individuals to be observed so that they understand what is going on and what you need. It will be helpful for them to be involved in developing the data collection sheet.
5. Develop a data collection sheet that will allow you to track the data required for decision making. It is always better to collect more data than to go back and start the collection process over because not enough information was collected initially.
6. If possible, decide how long you need to be observing your associates and how many observations you need to make. When more than one shift is involved, observations need to be taken on all shifts.
7. Compile results.
8. Determine how to present the data observed (for example, through graphs).
9. Review with management and associates the data from the observation (you may decide to post these data).

Teams will also want to interview and collect data from the customers. The checklist on page 162 can be used in compiling data.

CHECKLIST FOR CONSUMER SURVEYS

Elements	Results
1. We have identified our customers as:	
2. We have met with the customer(s) and together have identified their requirements and expectations to be:	
3. The areas of concern between us and our customers are:	
4. These areas of concern have been addressed in the following way:	
5. The criteria to measure our effectiveness in meeting the needs of the customer(s) have been identified as:	
6. When differences occur with the customer(s) we will use this procedure to resolve those differences:	
7. Roles to ensure that all individuals who deal with the customer directly and indirectly are as follows:	
8. These training programs have been identified or developed based on criteria established by the customer:	
9. Evaluation procedures based on the requirements of the customer(s) have been developed and are:	

COMMUNICATIONS AND CONFLICT

Team members can make meetings exciting by following these guidelines:

1. *Validate the other person's idea before adding your response.* Start by reinforcing the other person for offering the idea. That doesn't mean you agree completely, but it does convey that you value the other person's efforts and are interested in discussing the idea more.

2. *Avoid statements that convey blanket disagreement.* Even if you see problems, avoid making any opening statements that may discourage discussion of an idea's advantages and disadvantages.

3. *Don't discount the person offering the idea.* Don't start your response with any phrase that puts the other person down. That stops others from sharing ideas and often causes them to become defensive or even argumentative.

4. *Use* and *to connect your thoughts rather than* but *or* however. The words *but* and *however* discount what was just said. To convey that you meant your opening statement, connect it to your next thought using the word *and.*

5. *Build on the idea by adding what you like.* Add your thoughts about how the idea could be expanded, used in other ways, and perhaps even improved.

The team leader (or facilitator) should try to avoid dictating answers. If someone (Sally, for example) asks, "How can we cut costs?" the leader has several options for response.

Direct question: "Pat, what is one way to cut costs?"

Overhead question: "What are some ways we can cut costs?"

Return Question: "Sally, what do you think are some ways to cut costs?"

Relay Question: "Pat, how would you answer Sally's question about ways to cut costs?"

Sometimes a leader must intervene directly in the team process to get it back on track. Here are some reasons to intervene:

- No ideas
- Bogged down in the process
- Repetitive discussion
- Too many alternatives
- Lack of information
- Arguments over opinions
- Members have difficulty explaining their ideas
- Choices are/are not evident
- Team has difficulty evaluating ideas

In these instances an effective leader will:

- Call a "Stop Action"
- Describe what he or she has observed
- Confirm the observation with the team
- Help the group address and resolve the issue
- Conclude the intervention and maintain a focused team effort

Here are some simple tools for good team functioning:

Materials: A flip chart, pens, tape, a camera, handouts, notebooks, a timekeeper, items for positive reinforcement, training materials, video and audio equipment

Agendas: Don't put too much on the agenda. Start with the purpose of the meeting and then list the major discussion topics in order of discussion, assigning an amount of time to each topic and a person responsible for that topic. Allow time to review the minutes of last meeting, five minutes for feedback on "How we did," and five minutes at the end of the meeting for preparing the agenda for the next meeting. Don't change the agenda without the group's agreement. Post or distribute the agenda in advance of the meeting.

MEETING AGENDA SAMPLE FORM

This form needs to be prepared and distributed *prior* to each team meeting.

MEETING AGENDA

Team	Location	Date	Time

Team leader:
Purpose:
Anticipated Outcome:

Time	Topic	Responsibile Person

Distribution List:

Prepared by:

TEAM REPORTS

Team meeting reports provide team members, department associates, and management with information on what the team is working on. They record commitments so that each person on the team understands what is expected of her or him. They provide a systematic record of the continuous improvement process for the organization. The assignment and progress sheet is a good attachment to the team report to help the members meet their commitments and time frames.

The report ought to include the name of the group, the subject of the meeting, the names of those attending and those absent, the date, the time the meeting started, the subjects discussed and decisions made, responsibilities and assignments, the follow-up required, and the time the meeting ended.

Team reports need to be completed following each team meeting and distributed no later than forty-eight hours after the meeting has occurred.

It is not necessary to record every item that occurs in the meeting or what each person in the meeting does. The report is meant to record the highlights and should be written in a bulleted or numbered format for easy reading. It does not need to be a formalized minutes. One or two pages will be adequate.

Write in the past tense. Keep the minutes in the same order as the events of the meeting. Avoid blow-by-blow narratives and conversational style. Keep notes during the meeting and write them up later. Use information from flip charts. Attach an action sheet to the report when assignments are given. Ask for clarification during the meeting, if needed.

TEAM REPORT SAMPLE

P.O.D. PRIDE on Delivery
PRIDE Team Report
December 15, 9:00–10:30 A.M.
Training Room C
9th Meeting

PRIDE Team Members present: Kathy, Brian, Lisa, Debra, Shelly, Jim, Jody, Becky, Bill, Sandee

Members Absent: Bob, Vicki, Mark, Debbie

• Scribe: Lisa
• Timekeeper: Sandee
• Minutes: Brian

MEETING PROGRESSION:
1. Jill and Kim reviewed the minutes of the last meeting and introduced our guests—Bill and Kay.
2. A big thank-you from Jill was given to the entire team for all their efforts.
3. The second agenda topic we discussed was our current situation and the way it could be. Team members were given an Analysis Worksheet and were asked to send them to Kim by Monday, 12/20.
4. Team members requested Mark to address their concerns regarding coverage while the members are away from their desks for our meetings.
5. The team discussed how we will implement our tracking procedures.
    —Lisa handed out the Baseline Analysis tracking sheet and explained the format.
    —Brenda shared her idea of asking management to locate where information should be taken. She created a sample handout.

Break

6. See attached Actions for Continuous Improvement.
7. Our fifth agenda topic was how to begin charting results for our baseline.

Page 1

8. Last, we discussed our feedback and our next plan of action. The team members and guests said the following when asked what the team was proud of:

- Positive communication within all the departments.
- Our great leader, Jill. We all feel we can be open and discuss issues with her. She is also very helpful and offers support for the PRIDE team members. Good job, Jill.
- We are making much progress.
- Bonding and closeness.
- Management thinks we're doing great. The PRIDE team is making progress, and what we are doing will help everyone.
- Our teamwork—it's great everyone is volunteering for projects.
- We are bringing it all together as a team.
- The team is very focused.
- We have a better understanding of how/what each of us does to affect each others' jobs.
- Feel good about where we are—good pace.
- Great group—stimulating each other.

The team members also discussed these issues:

- Need to get management more directly involved.
- Overlap of pinpoints with other teams.
- Need to improve analysis process.
- Awareness of each other's difficulties.

9. Our next meeting will be 9:00 to 10:30 A.M. next Tuesday in Room C.

cc: PRIDE Team Members
President
VP of Sales
VP of Operations

ACTIONS FOR CONTINUOUS IMPROVEMENT SAMPLE FORM

This form is to be used when making assignments and should be attached to the PRIDE Team Report.

ACTIONS FOR CONTINUOUS IMPROVEMENT

Date: 12/15

Action to Be Taken	Person(s) Responsible	Due Date	Comments
Training on tracking procedures	Jill	12/29	
Meeting with management to review screen	Bill	12/17	
Update baseline tracking sheet	Lisa	12/20	
Pull files to be reviewed	Brenda/Lisa	12/18	
Create a list for each field	Deborah	12/17	
Info memo to management about teams needing to be away from desk	Becky	12/16	

EVALUATING TEAM MEMBERS FOR CONTINUOUS IMPROVEMENT

Teams need to evaluate their process at the end of each meeting. To provide a structure for evaluation to take place, you must create a mechanism for team members to talk openly and honestly about their perceptions and feelings of the meeting, and an opportunity for the team to practice continuous improvement in answering the question: *How can we make our team process more effective?*

Record responses on a flip chart and include them as part of the team report. Allow ten minutes for this at the end of every meeting. What went well? What might be done differently at the next meeting? How well did we work as a team? How well did we use the process?

Check Sheet for Team Leaders
Before the meeting

1. Be prepared.
   • Review notes from previous sessions.
   • Be sure everyone is notified of the meeting and receives an agenda.
   • Set goals for the meeting.
   • Check out facilities and materials needed *ahead* of time.
   • Prepare necessary materials.
   • Determine ways to give recognition and what kind of rewards you might use to reinforce behaviors during the session.
   • Follow up with individuals who have special assignments.
   • Set up the room so all physical barriers are removed and participants are at one table, not two tables set apart.

2. Create the right climate.

   • Greet people as they arrive.
   • Start on time.

During the Meeting
3. Reduce tension. Help people be comfortable.

   • Review the agenda so everyone will know what to expect.

- Allow for additions to the agenda.
- Set time frames.
- Create a relaxed climate.
- Create a climate of trust.
- State problems you hope to deal with in the form of questions.

4. Encourage discussion.

- Avoid singling anyone out.
- Provide an opportunity for everyone to speak.
- Speak of *us* and *we* rather than *you* and *I*.
- Watch out for hidden agendas—yours and others.
- Control dominating speakers.
- Avoid criticizing anyone's remarks.
- Focus on what *they* have to say, not on what *you* have to say.
- Give positive reinforcement generously.

5. Listen carefully.

- Concentrate on what a person is saying.
- Avoid giving your opinions. It is better to ask a question or give the group an opportunity to respond.
- Use open-ended/reflective questions.
- Listen carefully when someone proposes something different. Your goal is to get people to look at things in a different way.
- Keep off tangents.

6. Keep the discussion going.

- Ask questions: What if . . .? How might . . .?
- Encourage alternative ideas.
- Listen for ideas that lead to new ways of looking at things.

At the End of the Meeting

7. As you conclude the meeting
   • Have team critique the meeting

After the Meeting

8. Follow up.

   • See the that team report is distributed within twenty-four hours.
   • Check to see that team members are carrying out assignments.
   • Send a reminder notice of the next meeting.

TEAM CREATIVITY

Above all else, a team must be creative, innovative, and able to find new solutions. Here are some tips on creative discussion and problem solving:

   • The more ideas, the better
     —Wild ideas are welcome
     —No such thing as silly or stupid ideas
     —Think big
     —Don't wait
     —Quantity is important
   • Disagreement is OK
     —Conflict sometimes leads to better problem definition and solution generation
     —Center conflict on issues, not persons
   • Freewheeling and hitchhiking are good
     —Build on and spin off of each other's ideas
     —Let the mind go free

- Good listening skills are required
—Open-minded
—No ambushing
—The mind is like a parachute, it only works in an open position
—No interruptions, criticism, or judgmentalism
—Hear the discussion out
- Keep breaks to the time indicated
- Be open with opinions and feelings
—Participation is an absolute necessity
—Safe environment

As a leader or member of a team (or any organization), here are some things you can do to release the creativity within you:

- Define problems as broadly as possible during idea-generation stages.
- Delay evaluating your ideas until you have thought of a large number of alternatives.
- Avoid rigid, set patterns for doing things.
- Consider what the best conceivable outcome would be; temporarily ignore usual constraints on what can be done.
- Approach problems with a child's curiosity; ask questions; ask "How could this be better?"
- Be open and receptive to your own ideas and those of others.
- Spend time with creative people.
- Read magazines and books about unfamiliar topics; expose yourself to a wide range of different people and experiences.
- Don't accept your first "right" idea; think of as many as possible.
- Relax; allow time for incubation.

- Look for new relationships among ideas, not "right" and "wrong" answers.
- Take risks; forget about "failure."
- Recognize and avoid unwarranted assumptions.
- Visualize yourself being successful at whatever you are trying to create.
- Break larger problems into sub-problems and work on them one at a time.
- Set aside some time to practice creative thinking every day.
- Be flexible and persistent; keep trying different ideas until you find one that works.
- Eliminate barriers to creative thinking.

BARRIERS TO CREATIVE THINKING

Individual Barriers

- Inability to see a problem from various viewpoints
- Seeing what you expect to see; stereotyping
- Focusing on what is wrong with our own ideas and those of other people
- Evaluating our ideas at the same time we are generating them
- Inability to relax
- Lack of self-confidence; insecurity; fear
- Latching on to the first idea we think of
- Not taking enough time
- Lack of belief in one's own creative resources
- Fatigue; depression; stress; anger
- Lack of self-discipline
- Absence of commitment
- Inability to concentrate
- Fear of failure or of making mistakes
- Belief that fantasy and playfulness are a waste of time

- Unwillingness to tolerate ambiguity; desire for security, order

Organizational Barriers

- Myths that stifle creativity
  —Problem-solving is serious business; humor is out of place.
  —Reason, logic, numbers, and practicality are good; intuition, feelings, and qualitative judgments are bad.
  —Tradition is preferable to change.
  —Mistakes are bad and to be avoided.
- Overly "businesslike" atmosphere; discouragement of playfulness
- Organizational stress
- Lack of unscheduled time, perceived need for constant activity
- Crisis management; need to have everything done in a hurry
- Lack of structure and time to practice creative thinking
- Lack of reinforcement and rewards for creative efforts and ideas
- Lack of cooperation and trust
- An environment that allows for easy intrusions and many distractions
- Lack of structure and support for implementing ideas

Creativity Killers

These statements are creativity killers:

- Don't be ridiculous.
- Let's shelve it for right now.
- We're not ready for that.
- It won't work here.
- Our organization is different.
- Let's think about it some more.
- We did all right without it.

- It's too radical a change.
- The leaders won't like it.
- Where did you dig up that idea?
- It's not practical.
- We've never done it before.
- I have something better.
- It's too risky.
- Let's be sensible.
- We can't afford that.
- We'll never get it approved.
- It's good, but . . .
- Let's check on it later.
- Too much work.
- Let's get back to reality.
- That's been tried before.
- You can't be serious.

REACHING CONSENSUS

Once the creative juices have generated a range of ideas, the team must move toward consensus. Reaching consensus is the act of gaining general agreement. The team consensus may not be your first choice, but you willingly agree that you can and will support the team decision.

Consensus is not
  achieved through voting
  achieved by imposing a win-lose outcome
  dictating the conclusion
  simply giving in

Consensus is
  sharing ideas
  discussing, evaluating, and debating

organizing and prioritizing information

struggling to reach the best conclusion together

each person being open to the quiet leadership of his inner spirit

How important are teams? Let's return for a moment to the greatest leader in human history, Jesus of Nazareth. Jesus had a clear sense of His mission and purpose. There were literally thousands of things He might have done to carry out this mission. There was a whole world to reach. Just think of all the places He never went, the books He didn't write, the people He didn't help.

Instead, He spent 90 percent of His leadership time with twelve very unlikely, seemingly ordinary people. He met with them, challenged them, questioned them, nurtured them, corrected them, served as an example for them, and, above all, cared about them. One of them turned out to be a loser. But in the process of developing strong personal relationships with the disciples, the remaining eleven were forever changed in the inner spirit of their lives and personalities. Before they died, they broke the power of the Roman empire, reversed the course of human history, and turned the world upside down. That's the power of a team whose leader has tapped the inner spirit.

REFERENCES

1. Drew Lathin, "In the Midst of the Reengineering Forest," *The Journal for Quality and Participation*, January-February 1995, 59.
2. Carl E. Larson and Frank M. J. LaFasto, *Teamwork: What Can Go Wrong, What Must Go Right* (Newbury Park, Calif.: Sage, 1989), 8.

INDEX

Mother Teresa, 24–25, 56–57
Motivation, motivator, 28–41, 91, 92
  inner, 98
  and positive culture, 28
  testing, 31–33
Motorola, 17, 18, 61

Open-book management, 148
Organizations. *See also* Third Wave
  Organizations
  community-based, 57–58
  Corporate soul, 45
  and learning, 39, 48
  of the future, 62
  quality, 22–23
  purpose, 39, 56
  structure, 63–64, 67
Overconfidence, 123–24

Pay-at-risk, 96
Performance, 85–99
  compensation tied to, 29–35, 62,
    73, 88–89, 94–98
  improving, 27–38, 85–89, 106–7
  problems, 115–18, 121–22
  quality, laws of, 29, 33, 72, 85,
    87–88, 99
Pinpointing, pinpoints, 106–9, 111
Planning,
Praise, 73, 74, 87, 91, 94, 106
PRIDE
  management training program, 89
  problem-solving approach, 106,
    126
  quality improvement process,
    105–6
  teams, 61–62, 167–69
Problems
  analysis of, 103–11, 113–26, 160
  root causes of, 105, 118–22
  pinpointing, 106–11
  solving, 103–11, 113–26, 160,
    172–74
  solving by teams, 103, 155, 158,
    160, 172–74, 175
Problems, types of
  attitude, 115–16, 117
  knowledge, 115–16
  performance, 115
  skill, 115, 116–17
  system, 115–16, 118
  work flow, 120–22
Process analysis

flow charting, 120
  mapping, 120–21
Productivity
  goals for, 32, 34
  improving, 32
Profit sharing, 23
  and productivity, 33–34
Psychology, 35
Punishment, 48, 72, 78–80, 89

Quality, 15–25, 105, 108–111. *See
  also*
Total Quality Management (TQM)
  attitude, 27
  circles, 152
  companies and organizations,
    17–18, 21–23
  and culture of company, 21, 28, 98
    109, 152
  control, 86, 102
  customer's perception of, 17–18
  and customer service, 16, 18–20
  defined by the customer, 15, 16,
    18–19, 21, 22, 23, 109
  defined by the organization, 15
  customer-oriented, 18
  employee-driven, 105, 110
  lack of, 18–19
  movement, 15
  performance, laws of, 29, 33, 72,
    85, 87–88, 99
  processes, 110
  and profits, 17–18
  programs, 15, 27–28, 110
  teams, 133, 152
  total, 21, 152
Quantity, 67, 108–9

Recognition, 73, 74, 87, 88, 91, 94, 98
  Team-based, 35
Reengineering, 58–67
  process, 59, 60, 120–21
  success stories, 58–62
  systems, 118
Reinforcement
  and behavior, 43
  and improvement, 76, 93
  financial, 94-96, 106
  knowledgeable, 73, 91
  and performance, 29, 31, 34, 74,
    76, 78, 88–89, 94–95
  personalized, 75, 91
  specific, 92–94

systems issues, 65
timely, 33, 74, 92
Reinforcement, types of
immediate (timely), 74, 92
intangible, 73, 88, 91, 93
negative, 72, 75–76
positive, 29, 72–75, 76, 78, 80, 85,
91, 93, 106–7, 171
tangible, 73, 75, 88, 91, 93
team-based, 35
Reinforcers
intangible, 88, 91, 94–95, 96, 106
positive, 91
selecting effective, 89–90
tangible, 88, 91, 96
Rewards, 29, 66, 89, 96–99. *See also*
Praise; Recognition
and behavior, 28–34, 62, 72, 76,
85–89, 92–93, 99
examples of, 73, 74, 85–87, 90, 92,
96–97
financial, 31, 94–95, 106
immediate, 92
and improvement, 29, 85–99, 106,
107, 125
intangible, 73, 88, 89, 96
spiritual, 98–99
tangible, 96
Ritz-Carlton, 18, 22
Root cause. *See* Analysis

S. S. Kresge Company, 103
Self-esteem 40, 62
ServiceMaster, 46
Skinner, B. F., 35–36, 37
Slogans, 133
Solectron, 17, 18
Steinmetz, Charles, 113–14
Strategic planning and direction, 67,
129–30, 141

Team(s). *See also* Creativity;
Problems; Teamwork
assumptions, 153
atmosphere, 154
champions, 157–58
cross-functional, 61, 165
and culture of company, 152
data collection by, 160–62
decisions, 158, 159–60, 176
facilitator and coach, 157, 163
goals, 154, 158
leaders, leadership, 40, 151, 155,

157, 158, 163–64, 170–72, 177
and learning, 48
meetings, 155, 159, 163–66,
170–72
members, 158, 163
outstanding, 154
PRIDE, 61–62, 167–69
process, 158, 159, 163, 169
recognition, 35
responsibilities, 158
report, 166–69
and reward systems, 33–35, 65, 66,
153
rules, 154, 159–60
skills, 153
and systems of company, 65
and work processes, 65–66
Teamwork, 34–35
Termination, 78–80
Texas Instruments, 17
Third Wave Organizations, 63
Time
logs, 119
management, 115
Timeliness, 108, 109, 110
Total Quality Management (TQM),
25, 43, 82, 94, 110–11
Toyoda, Kiichiro, 126
Toyota, 34, 126
Travelers Insurance, 23
Trust, 28, 31, 126, 171, 175

UtiliCorp, 61–62

Values, 45, 135–38, 147
Vision
corporate, 131
leaders shaping, 45
spiritual, 45
statement, 25, 60
shared, 147

W. T. Grant Company, 103
Wainwright Industries, 130
Walton, Sam, 104
Weaknesses, identifying, 120–21
Westinghouse Electric, 17, 21
Work, measures of, 108
Work flow diagrams, 120

Xerox, 17

Zytec Corporation, 17

If you are interested in information about other books
written from a biblical perspective,
please write to the following address:

Northfield Publishing
215 West Locust Street
Chicago, IL 60610